The Essential Poetry of
Bohdan Ihor Antonych

Volodymyr Lasovs'kyi, *Portrait of Bohdan Ihor Antonych*, oil on canvas, 1936. Courtesy of Litopys Publishers.

The Essential Poetry of Bohdan Ihor Antonych

Ecstasies and Elegies

TRANSLATED FROM THE UKRAINIAN
BY MICHAEL M. NAYDAN

With an Introduction by Lidia Stefanowska

BUCKNELL
UNIVERSITY PRESS

Lewisburg, Pennsylvania

First paperback edition 2024
ISBN 978-1-68448-530-7

The Library of Congress has cataloged the hardcover edition as follows:

Library of Congress Cataloging-in-Publication Data
Antonych, Bohdan-Ihor, 1909–1937.
[Poems. English. Selections]
The essential poetry of Bohdan Ihor Antonych : ecstasies and elegies / translated from
Ukrainian by Michael M. Naydan ; with an introduction by Lidia Stefanowska.
p. cm.
Includes bibliographical references.
ISBN 978-0-8387-5769-7 (alk. paper)
1. Antonych, Bohdan-Ihor, 1909–1937—Translations into English. I. Naydan,
Michael M., 1952–II. Title.
PG3948.A637A2 2010
891.79'13 2009050387

A British Cataloging-in-Publication record for this book
is available from the British Library.

References to internet websites (URLs) were accurate at the time of writing. Neither
the author nor Bucknell University Press is responsible for URLs that may have
expired or changed since the manuscript was prepared.

♾ The paper used in this publication meets the requirements of the American
National Standard for Information Sciences—Permanence of Paper for Printed
Library Materials, ANSI Z39.48–1992.

bucknelluniversitypress.org

Distributed worldwide by Rutgers University Press

For a wonderful friend, Nadya N,
who walks the poetry road

Contents

Part III: From the Collection
The Book of the Lion (1936)

Part IV: From the Collection
The Green Gospel (1938)
FIRST CHAPTER

FIRST LYRIC INTERMEZZO

SECOND CHAPTER

SECOND LYRIC INTERMEZZO

Part V: From the Collection
Rotations (1938)

Part VI: From Poetry Not Published in Collections

Part VII: From the Collection
A Welcome to Life (1931)

Acknowledgments

The poems "Musica Noctis," "De Morte I," "Ars Poetica 1" and "Liber Peregrinorum 3" were previously published in *The Grand Harmony* (Lviv: Litopys Publishers, 2007). The poems "Self-Portrait" and "Six Strophes of Mysticism" appeared in *A Bilingual Anthology of Twentieth-Century Ukrainian Poetry* (Lviv: Litopys Publishers, 2000). And "Three Rings," "The Village," "The Green Gospel," "A Night on St. George's Square," "A Song on the Indestructibility of Matter," and "Green Faith" have previously been published in Number 19 of *The Dirty Goat* (Fall 2008). I am also extremely grateful to Mykhailo Komarnytsky, Director of Litopys Publishers of Lviv, Ukraine, for kindly providing the digital photographical illustration for the volume from his *Povne zibrannia tvoriv* (2009) complete works edition of Antonych's poetry.

A Note on the Translation

MICHAEL M. NAYDAN

The extraordinary Lemko-Ukrainian poet and literary critic Bohdan Ihor Antonych lived on this earth for just a brief twenty-eight years, from 1909 to 1937. Yet despite his young age and premature death, he managed to create an extraordinarily powerful and innovative poetry. In the opinion of many who intimately know his works, he should be placed in the same lofty heights as contemporaries such as Rainer Maria Rilke, T. S. Eliot, Federico García Lorca, and Czeslaw Miłosz. Critics have also compared him to Walt Whitman and Dylan Thomas, the former for his nature poetry and the latter for his profound engagement with the theme of human mortality. Yet because of Antonych's early demise and the fact that he wrote in Ukrainian, a language whose identity has been submerged in other empires (Polish, Austro-Hungarian, tsarist, and Soviet), he has not achieved greater acclaim. Remarkably little is known about Antonych as more mysteries than facts abound regarding his life.

Little of Antonych's works has been available in English translation. The émigré Ukrainian poet Bohdan Boychuk published a small but well-received book of Antonych's selected poetry in the English translations of American poets Mark Rudman and Paul Nemser under the title *A Square of Angels* (Ann Arbor: Ardis Publishers, 1977). That volume contains an exceptional introduction by Bohdan Rubchak. To honor Antonych on the hundredth anniversary of his birth, I have translated for this edition a number of additional poems from Antonych's poetry to complement that first volume. Thus, over half of these translations are appearing in English for the first time, and my versions also provide my own interpretations of previously translated works. This compilation includes selections from all six of Antonych's collections as well as from works appearing outside of them.

I have chosen not to use a completely chronological approach in presenting Antonych's poetry in this volume but rather to foreground his best works from *The Grand Harmony* (*Velyka harmoniia*, 1932–33), *Three Rings* (*Try persteni*, 1934), *The Book of the Lion* (*Knyha Leva*, 1936), *The Green Gospel* (*Zelena Ievanheliia*, 1938), *Rotations* (*Rotatsii*, 1938), and poetry published outside of these collections. Selections from his earliest collection, *A Welcome to Life* (Pryvitannia zhyttia, 1931), that retrospectively shows the formative stage of the poet's development, will appear at the end of the volume.

Antonych's poetry presents myriad problems for the translator, particularly in the area of syntax, where variant readings are possible as a result of the more malleable nature of his poetic style that is rife with inversion. Rhythmical features are translated whenever possible but are not adhered to slavishly. Rhyme is also not presented in my translations in an exact way but is used occasionally where it can occur in a natural way. I have tried my best to maintain the rich imagery that is a hallmark of Antonych's poetry. I have also kept footnotes to the poems at a minimum so as not to impede the reader's aesthetic experience of reading the poetry.

I am especially grateful to Yuri Andrukhovych for sharing his expertise with me in choosing the selections for this anniversary volume. While my selections partly reflect a volume of Antonych's poems that Yuri helped to select, translate, and publish in German, my final selections differ somewhat from that volume, with a larger number of poems having been translated. Other differences reflect my personal interests in certain aspects of Antonych's work.

Special thanks to Lidia Stefanowska for sharing with me so much of her expertise and insight on Antonych and also for providing such a thorough and thoughtful introduction to the volume. I owe a large debt of gratitude to Olha Tytarenko for her invaluable advice in combing through the manuscript for errors in translation and for increasing my understanding of the complexities of Antonych's poetry. Many thanks also to Linda Ivanits and to my daughter Lila Naydan for their extremely useful suggestions for emendations in my biographical sketch of the poet. I alone, of course, am responsible for any errors or omissions.

A Biographical Sketch of the Poet

MICHAEL M. NAYDAN

Biographical resources on Bohdan Ihor Antonych are extraordinarily scant, particularly when one considers his enormous poetic talent. Perhaps the upheaval caused by the Nazi and Soviet armies that alternately occupied the city of Lviv just a few years after Antonych's death in 1937 were partly to blame for scattering those who knew him well and preventing them from publishing more about his life. From the few extant photographs of Antonych, we see him dressed mostly in a bow tie with dark round glasses and hair slicked back in the style of the time. He had the look of a quiet, reserved intellectual, something akin to the appearance of his American contemporary T. S. Eliot, (especially when Eliot wore his glasses), though Eliot had leaner facial features and Antonych a wider brow. In the introduction to his edition of Antonych's poetry, *Collected Works* (*Zibrani tvory*, 1967), the poet and artist Sviatoslav Hordynsky comments on the striking contrast between the real Antonych and the image of his poetic persona: "With his large head, in his glasses, he looked like a real intellectual, but in his everyday life he would sooner have peace and comfort, which he needed for his perpetual contemplation" (Hordynsky 16).[1] The artist Volodymyr Lasovs'kyi, Antonych's friend from his university days, underscores the "dualism" of what he calls "the two faces

---

1 All translations from Ukrainian and Slovak sources in this biographical sketch are mine.

of Antonych"—one the image of poetic bravura, the other quite ordinary (Lasovs'kyi 296). He further highlights Antonych's unremarkable appearance as follows: "His long, slightly weak fingers in a handshake, his slightly heavyset stature with a tendency to gain weight, the prematurely balding head of an intellectual, his small, cracked lips, sometimes broken out from a fever" (Lasovs'kyi 297).

The most detailed information on Antonych comes from a handful of brief memoirs by his fiancée Ol'ha Oliinyk (published first under her maiden name and later under her married name Ksenzhopol's'ka); a few family members including his maternal uncle, Oleksandr Voloshynovych; and friends such as Sviatoslav Hordynsky, who managed to keep manuscripts of Antonych's writings for the publication of a single-volume collected-works edition of the poet's writings in 1967. Several of these memoirs were collected in a volume commemorating the thirtieth anniversary of Antonych's death entitled *The Rings of Youth* (*Persteni molodosti*) that was published in Bratislava, Slovakia in 1966.

Antonych was born on October 5, 1909, in the village of Nowica in the Lemko region of what is now in Poland. Ukrainian poet and scholar Dmytro Pavlychko describes Nowica as a "picturesque mountain village. Pasture lands, fields and gardens on the slopes of the mountains, dark blue fir trees, gurgling brooks, ravines and streams—the landscapes extolled by Antonych are a reality here" ("Nezhasaiushchyi persten'zhyttia"). Antonych was the son of a village Byzantine-Rite Greek-Catholic priest, Vasyl Kit, who changed the family's last name (meaning "tomcat") to the more sedate Antonych shortly before the poet was born. The boy grew up speaking Polish along with the Lemko dialect of Ukrainian, which contrasts with standard spoken and literary Ukrainian by virtue of its different syllabic stress and its dialectal locutions. The poet acquired literary Ukrainian, the language of his poetry, during his schooling and later in life. According to Ol'ha Oliinyk, Antonych's interest in poetry was nurtured by his nanny, a young village girl, who constantly read poetry to him, told him fairy tales, and sang songs (Oliinyk 291). The young Antonych would ask her to repeat poems that he particularly liked until he learned them by heart (Oliinyk 291; Ksenzhopol's'ka 302). We know, too, from various sources that the young Antonych was a shy, quiet, and introspective child: these aspects of his personality accompanied him throughout his life.

In order to escape from their war-torn region, the family moved to Vienna, where they lived from 1914 to 1919. They suffered considerable privations during the war years but managed to survive. His fiancée tells one particular story that he would often repeat to her about his childhood days in Vienna. She feels that it impacted him profoundly. While playing with a group of children in a park, the young Antonych somehow lost his mother. He ended up returning home alone to his father by following landmarks he remembered while wandering through the city and by hugging closely to walls in order to avoid the traffic in the streets (Oliinyk 291–292).

Polish authorities arrested Antonych's father in 1919 for political activities. At that time Antonych and his mother moved to Pryashiv (now called Presov and located in Slovakia) to live with her brother, who was soon condemned to death by the Polish Pilsudsky government for his activities in support of the transfer of the Galician part of the Lemko region to Czechoslovakian rule (Pavlychko, "Pisnia pro neznyshchennist' materii" 9). Both Antonych's father and brother were later released.

Antonych was a frail and sickly child. His uncle, Oleksandr Voloshynovych, mentions that at the age of ten, when the boy had come to live with him, he was constantly tired and feverish (Voloshynovych 307). A private teacher homeschooled Antonych until the age of eleven. His tutor thought extremely highly of him, and the young Antonych would often borrow books from her (Oliinyk 292). In 1919 he entered Queen Sophia State Gymnasium in Sanok, the only Polish school in the Lemko region at the time. During his eight years of school, he focused on the study of Greek and Latin, along with two hours per week of Ukrainian language instruction. Antonych befriended several Ukrainian boys he met at the gymnasium, which led to a nurturing of his interest in the Ukrainian language and literature.

During 1923–1925, while still at the gymnasium, Antonych began writing. His teacher of Ukrainian for his last two years was the Ukrainian artist Lev Hets, who had a particularly profound influence on Antonych. Hets recalls that Antonych was "a very calm, quiet" boy, who "often was pensive, thoughtful" (Hets 306). Antonych was also active in the school's choir and learned to play the violin. At school he performed in concerts and composed several songs, including a march performed by the entire school. He also had a particular interest in art and began to paint at that time.

Antonych's father and mother moved to the village of Bortniantyn about fifty kilometers west of the city of Lviv in 1925 where his father became pastor of the Greek-Catholic Church of the Dormition of the Holy Mother (Stryzhevs'ka). In 1928 Antonych completed his studies at the gymnasium with distinction and enrolled at Lviv University in western Ukraine, which at that time was under Polish rule. At the university, he specialized in Polish and Ukrainian philology.

He began to publish in local Lviv journals in 1931. His first collection of juvenilia appeared in a publication series of the journal *Dazhboh* (the name of one of the ancient Slavic gods) under the title *A Welcome to Life* (*Pryvitannia zhyttia*). The poems in this collection represent Antonych's unbridled youthful romanticism and first attempts at learning the rules of versification in his newly acquired literary language. While in retrospect we can see that the collection was not a great aesthetic success, its publication earned him accolades and set him firmly on the path to becoming a professional poet. He actively participated in student life at the university, particularly with the Student Circle of Ukrainianists, which organized literary, artistic, and musical activities. Antonych, according to his classmate Volodymyr Barahura, shied away from women because of his timid nature, but he met his first love, Lida, at meetings of the Ukrainian student organization (Hordynsky 9). The romance, however, was short-lived. In his university studies Antonych distinguished himself among his peers and became the favorite student of Professor Gertner, who had hoped to send him abroad on a government-funded stipend to further his studies. The plan, however, never materialized.

Over the course of 1932–1933 Antonych wrote the poems for *The Grand Harmony* (*Velyka harmoniia*), which was never published as a collection in his lifetime, although seven of the poems appeared in the Catholic journal *Bells* (*Dzvony*) in 1932 and 1933. The poetry of *The Grand Harmony* comprises Antonych's meditations on the nature of God and focuses on Antonych's beliefs as well as his doubts. The poems represent a significant aesthetic step in his poetic development from his first collection, with several particularly impressive poems such as "Musica Noctis," "De Morte I" and "Liber Peregrinorum."

In 1933 Antonych received his master of philosophy degree in Slavic philology and, according to his fiancée, began to prepare himself to work on a doctorate. In 1934 he published his poems in the Western Ukrainian journals *Fires* (*Vohni*), *Meeting* (*Nazustrich*), and *We* (*My*). Through the financial support of Bohdan Kravtsiv, he published his first mature collection of poetry, *Three Rings* (*Try persteni*), for which he received the literary prize of the Ivan Franko Society of Ukrainian Writers and Journalists. The publication of the volume unequivocally established his reputation as a masterful poet. Particularly noteworthy in the collection are his poems "Self-Portrait," "Three Rings," his various elegies ("An Elegy about a Singing Door," "An Elegy about the Keys of Love," "An Elegy about the Ring of a Song," "An Elegy about the Ring of Youth"), and "Night on St. George Square."

Over the course of the next three years he prepared four books of poetry for publication, wrote numerous articles and shorter prose works, and began work on a novel as well as a libretto for an opera by the well-known Ukrainian composer Antin Rudnytsky. In 1936 he published his collection *The Book of the Lion* (*Knyha Leva*), arguably his finest collection, which contains such masterpieces of meditative poetry as "A Song about the Light before Time," "Six Strophes of Mysticism," "A Square of Angels," and "A Song on the Indestructibility of Matter."

He met his fiancée-to-be, Ol'ha Oliinyk, in 1934, but was never to marry her because of his premature death. Oliinyk had come to Lviv on vacation to visit friends and first encountered him in the

Oasis Sweet Shop on Rus Street in the center of the city. She found him to be "smiling goodheartedly, polite, sincere, without any agitated gestures, calm and very sober-minded in conversation" (Ksenzhopol's'ka 301). She adds the following to her description of him: "His green eyes gaze seriously through his eyeglasses and brighten up when he smiles. Sometimes it seems they see not only everything visible, but even what will be. He converses with me so joyfully that I feel as though we've been acquainted for a long time, and it was not just the fact that we weren't strangers, but even more—we were simply friends" (Ksenzhopol's'ka 301). The two intended to marry sometime in 1938. The manuscript for his collection *The Green Gospel* (*Zelena Ievanheliia*), planned for publication in the same year, was to bear a dedication to his wife.

Antonych's fiancée gives a detailed description of his poetic method in one of her reminiscences of him.

> Normally he would write every other day. Usually in the morning. He would jot down individual phrases, then build the entire whole. He would take a stick in his hands and walk about the room, scanning or singing some melody. Later he would write down the poem from the separate phrases—or just part of it—and would continue to pace about the room. He loved to rhythmically tap with his stick while this was going on. It often happened that in the morning he would write down an entire poem right away—and these mostly required no changes.
> "You know, sometimes I have the impression as though someone has whispered something in my ear. Literally whispered." That's what he related to me about his poetic inspiration (Oliinyk 294)

His friend Volodymyr Lasovs'kyi describes Antonych's method of writing as a "dream-creative process" (*snotvornyi protses*): "In the morning the half-asleep Antonych would put on his glasses, rise up from the bed, and sit down at a wobbly little desk to hastily write down the poetry that had blossomed in his dreams" (Lasovs'kyi 296).

In June 1937, at the pinnacle of his aesthetic development as a poet, Antonych took ill and eventually underwent an operation for appendicitis. During his illness, while he was too weak to write himself, he dictated changes to the manuscript of the opera *Dovbush* to his fiancée and had plans to complete it on vacation after his recovery. Through complications of the surgery and after contracting pneumonia, he died of heart failure on July 6, 1937. He was buried on July 7 in the Yaniv Cemetery on the outskirts of the city of Lviv, amid the verdant world of nature that had been such a source of inspiration for him and a hallmark of his poetry. His collections *The Green Gospel* (*Zelena Ievanheliia*) and *Rotations* (*Rotatsii*) appeared posthumously in 1938. *The Green Gospel* contains a significant amount of nature poetry, while the brief collection *Rotations* is comprised of urban poetry with apocalyptic motifs, the latter perhaps a poetic vision and premonition of the Nazi and Soviet invasions that were to come.

Antonych's father died in 1945 in the village of Bortiantyn just after the Soviets had annexed that part of Ukraine from Poland. Shortly thereafter, all Ukrainian Greek-Catholic priests were arrested or imprisoned at Stalin's orders, and the Antonych home was confiscated by authorities. Antonych's mother lived for another decade until her death in the house of one of her neighbors in the village (Stryzhevs'ka).

The impact and influence of Antonych on future generations of Ukrainian writers—particularly on contemporary luminaries such as Yuri Andrukhovych and Viktor Neborak—has been phenomenal. Andrukhovych's novel *The Twelve Rings* (*Dvanadtsiat' obruchiv*), in fact, is based to a great degree on Antonych's life. The great poetry that Antonych created certainly will outlive his all-too-brief life for generations to come.

Reference List

Antonych, Bohdan Ihor. 1966. *Persteni molodosti*. Ed. Mykola Neverli. Bratislava: Slovats'ke pedahohichne vydavnytsvo v Bratislavi.

Antonych, Bohdan Ihor. 2003. *Vybrane*. Ed. M.N. Moskalenko. Kyiv: Vydavnytsvo "Kyivs'ka Pravda."

Hets, Lev. 1966. "Shcho zhaduiu ia pro B. I. Antonycha?" In *Persteni molodosti*, ed. Mykola Neverli, 306. Bratislava: Slovats'ke pedahohichne vydavnytsvo v Bratislavi.

Hordynsky, Sviatoslav. 1967. "Bohdan Ihor Antonych: Ioho zhyttia i tvorchist'." In *Zibrani tvory*, ed. Sviatoslav Hordynsky and Bohdan Rubchak, 7–26. Winnipeg: Organization for Defense of Lemkivshchyna in America.

Il'nyts'kyi, Mykola. 1991. *Bohdan-Ihor Antonych: Literaturnyi portret*. Kyiv: Radians'kii pys'mennyk.

Ksenzhopol's'ka, Ol'ha. 1966. "Zabutyi poet Lemkivshchyny." In *Persteni molodosti*, ed. Mykola Neverli, 300–5. Bratislava: Slovats'ke pedahohichne vydavnytsvo v Bratislavi.

Kuzelova-Neubauerova, Anna. 1966. "Hrstka vzpominek na Bohdana." In *Persteni molodosti*, ed. Mykola Neverli, 308–9. Bratislava: Slovats'ke pedahohichne vydavnytsvo v Bratislavi.

Lasovs'kyi, Volodymyr. 1966. "Dva oblychchia Antonycha." In *Persteni molodosti*, ed. Mykola Neverli, 296–300. Bratislava: Slovats'ke pedahohichne vydavnytsvo v Bratislavi.

Novikova, Maryna. 2003. "Mifosvit Antonycha." In Bohdan Ihor Antonych: *Vybrane*, ed. M.N. Moskalenko, 5–18. Kyiv: Vydavnytsvo "Kyivs'ka Pravda."

Oliinyk, Ol'ha. 1966. "Nadhrobok na mohyli shchastia." In *Persteni molodosti*, ed. Mykola Neverli, 291–96. Bratislava: Slovats'ke pedahohichne vydavnytsvo v Bratislavi.

Pavlychko, Dmytro. 1967. "Pisnia pro neznyshchennist' materii." In *Pisnia pro neznyshchennist' materii: poezii*, ed. Dmytro Pavlychko, 7–26. Kyiv: Radians'kyi pys'mennyk.

———. "Nezhasaiushchyi persten' zhyttia." http://virchi.narod.ru/poeziya/antonich-zmisth.htm.

Rubchak, Bohdan. 1975. "Antonych Grows. The Grass Grows." In *Square of Angels: Selected Poems*. Trans. Mark Rudman and Paul Nemser with Bohdan Boychuk, ix–xx. Ann Arbor: Ardis Publishers.

Stefanowska, Lidia. 2006. *Antonych, Antynomii*. Kyiv: Chasopys "Krytyka."

Stryzhevs'ka, Iryna. "U rodynnomu hnizdi Bohdana-Ihoria Antonycha. *Lvivs'ka hazeta*" no. 152 (October 16, 2008), http://www.gazeta.lviv.ua/articles/2008/10/16/35198.

Voloshynovych, Oleksandr. 1966. "Spomienky na mojho synovca a jeho rodicov." In *Persteni molodosti*, ed. Mykola Neverli, 306–8. Bratislava: Slovats'ke pedahohichne vydavnytsvo v Bratislavi.

http://uk.wikipedia.org/wiki/Антонич_Богдан-Ігор_Васильович.

http://www.ukrlib.com.ua/bio/printout.php?id=10.

Between Creation and the Apocalypse
THE POETRY OF BOHDAN IHOR ANTONYCH

LIDIA STEFANOWSKA

Bohdan Ihor Antonych was one of the most remarkable modernist Ukrainian poets of the twentieth century. He left an extraordinary literary legacy with just a handful of books of published poetry despite his premature death at the age of twenty-eight in 1937. He was a poet, literary critic, translator, and journalist. Antonych's formal education, at the gymnasium in Sanok and at Lviv University (1928–34), was conducted exclusively in Polish. At home he spoke Lemko, a Ruthenian dialect customarily grouped with Ukrainian, but distinctly different from the literary language (the primary differences are in stress, intonation, and vocabulary, features especially important in prosody). As for literary Ukrainian, which became the language of his writing, Antonych began to learn it relatively late as a teenager at the gymnasium. Literary bilingualism and biculturalism were formative aspects in his artistic development. For this reason, Antonych's literary oeuvre requires a proper understanding of his particular cultural and linguistic milieu that takes into account the complicated interaction of three distinct elements: his Lemko origins, his formal Polish education, and his relatively late embrace of literary Ukrainian. These features had a great impact on his writings.

There are parallels between Antonych's biculturalism and that of other Ukrainian writers. The fin de siècle prose writer Olha Kobylanska, for example, grew up in Bukovyna. Educated in

German schools, she first wrote in the language of her schooling, which later led her to introduce the ideas of certain German writers into Ukrainian literature (Nietzsche and Goethe, for instance). Antonych can also be compared to the Ukrainian Neoclassicists (for example, Mykola Zerov and Mykhailo Drai-Khmara) who, in the Soviet-controlled eastern half of Ukraine, wrote their first poems in Russian. Although Antonych never actually wrote in Polish, the comparison with these other bilingual poets is nevertheless useful since, like Antonych, each of them drew upon a multicultural heritage and from it brought into Ukrainian literature certain new aesthetic ideas.

After the First World War Ukraine was divided among Poland, the Soviet Union, Czechoslovakia, and Romania. In the western territories the development of Ukrainian language, education, and literature was hindered to a greater or lesser degree by various government measures. Yet, relatively speaking, these areas enjoyed greater creative freedom and an absence of direct political control—unlike the case in Soviet Ukraine. The most advanced area in many respects was Halychyna (Galicia) under Polish rule, with its capital city of Lviv (Lwow in Polish). When the growth of modern culture in Soviet Ukraine came to a halt with the imposition of Stalinist controls, Lviv was ready to take over the leadership of Ukrainian intellectual life since its intellectuals had the advantage of free access to western European culture.

From the outset of Antonych's literary career, in the context of western Ukrainian literature, his poetry had a different sound and texture to it. His literary interests were unconventional for his milieu: he concerned himself with the metaphysical, philosophical, and metapoetic. He was, moreover, the only Ukrainian poet at the time who wrote theoretical articles on new concepts of poetic language and introduced a new artistic experience and formulated his own literary agenda, addressing a new implied reader. All of this reflected not just a lively creative talent, but one informed with a fusion of two cultural traditions, able to transcend the limitations of the western Ukrainian literary canon of the time by the introduction of universal artistic values. And it is for its universal qualities that Antonych's poetry is still quite prominent, with a great impact on the writing of three different literary generations, embodied in poets such as Ihor Kalynets (who debuted in the 1960s), Ihor Rymaruk (1970s), and Yuri Andrukhovych and Viktor Neborak (1980s).

Antonych's literary activity began with contributions to student periodicals in 1928–30. However, he first drew the attention of literary critics in 1931 with the publication of *A Welcome to Life* (*Pryvitannia zhyttia*), his first book of poetry. There followed a period in his career for the next year or so when he plunged into religious contemplation and perceived the role of the poet as an instrument of God's will, as understood within his Christian upbringing. In 1932 he wrote a number of religious poems and published several of them in the Greek-Catholic journal *Bells* (*Dzvony*.) The collection was published only posthumously in an American edition of his *Collected Works* (*Zibrani tvory*) in 1967 under the title *The Grand Harmony* (*Velyka harmoniia*). These poems have been translated into English by Michael Naydan and published by Litopys Publishers in a bilingual edition in 2007.

Real success arrived with the appearance of Antonych's next book, *Three Rings* (*Try persteni*), which was published in 1934 and earned the prestigious literary prize of the Society of Writers and Journalists. From this moment on, Antonych began to be considered among the best of the youngest generation of Ukrainian poets. In 1936 *The Book of the Lion* (*Knyha Leva*) appeared, bringing him another literary award and encomia from the most prominent Ukrainian critics. Oleh Olzhych at that time pronounced Antonych the best Ukrainian poet of his time. Simultaneous to *The Book of the Lion*, Antonych had been working on two other books, *The Green Gospel* (*Zelena Ievanheliia*) and *Rotations* (*Rotatsii*). Both were published posthumously in 1938.

Antonych was only twenty-one when his first volume was published. As is the case with many young writers, *A Welcome to Life* had a certain stiff and clumsy quality to it. Nevertheless, his debut came as a great surprise to critics and readers, who were astounded by the abundance of new poetic themes (for example, sports and the unconscious) never before expressed in the poetry of Ukrainian Galicia. His early poetry is characterized by alliterative orchestration, novelty of rhyme, lexical and rhythmic variety—from free verse to games with the sonnet form, from direct visual imagery to verbal metaphors, bordering on baroque-like conceits. The critics welcomed him warmly, and from the outset he became a subject of their close interest. Yet it is striking that all of his contemporary commentators employed conservative methods of interpretation, which failed to perceive and describe the innovative nature of his poetic diction adequately. From this arose many misunderstandings in the interpretation of Antonych's work. In general, critics praised him for his pastoral vision of nature, a theme familiar to the Ukrainian reader, and ultimately classified him, as Ievhen Malaniuk puts it, as a "poet of the earth." Yet when in his later work Antonych turned to different motifs (for instance, the theme of the city) and no longer fit the label of "poet of the earth," Malaniuk asserted that Antonych's dark imagery, which prevails in his urban poetry, mainly represented in the book *Rotations*, results from "the complex of a former peasant." This unfortunate evaluation by Malaniuk gave rise to a tradition that perceives Antonych as a poet of nature for whom the urban theme by definition is alien and artificial, a perception which lasts to the present day in many circles.

It is true that at the time of Antonych's writing the theme of the city was still quite novel in Ukrainian literature. This is perhaps the main reason that led the Ukrainian critics to interpret any negative representation of urban life as the psychological reaction of a peasant recoiling from the harsh and unfamiliar city. In the case of Antonych, however, this interpretation is not quite right. It fails, first of all, to accord several biographical facts. Antonych's youth was spent primarily in urban or semi-urban settings, and his formative experience was not primarily that of a rural person. More importantly, the argument does not touch on the real, much more fundamental issue—Antonych's "otherness" in the Ukrainian setting, which stems from his liminal cultural position. From this viewpoint, his urban thematics and his tendency toward a vision of catastrophe in his mature writing cannot properly be understood in an exclusively Ukrainian context or compared to the typical Ukrainian writer. It must be seen as the result of his different cultural experience. Antonych's early works reflect not the "complex of the peasant," but rather his Polish education and cultural heritage, where the urban theme was by no means new. For this reason Antonych should be compared not to such Ukrainian writers as Pidmohylny, but rather with such Polish poets as Czeslaw Miłosz and Józef Czechowicz, whose catastrophic mode of expression revealed the general atmosphere of crisis and mood of existential anxiety that prevailed in Europe in the 1930s.

Antonych's life ended in 1937, at the age of only twenty-eight. Yet even before his untimely death, he had achieved an astonishing artistic maturity. Only six years separated his first volume from his last. Nevertheless, within that time he had written five books of poetry (not including *The Grand Harmony*). His first two books, *A Welcome to Life* and *Three Rings*, reflect a different emotional and poetic stage in comparison to the three later volumes—*The Book of the Lion*, *A Green Gospel*, and the unfinished collection *Rotations*. In his debut book Antonych had already introduced almost all the themes that would interest him for the remainder of his life, but they were handled in a manner that was naive and unconvincing. A mere four years later, he was already able to elaborate on them, using a mature and original diction that differed significantly from that of the average western Ukrainian writer of the period. Feeling an aversion to the traditionalism (especially realism and nationalism) of most Ukrainian writers and an aversion to the constraints of ideological orthodoxies, Antonych went on his own path. He valued only a handful of contemporary Ukrainian poets: the early Pavlo Tychyna, the early Mykola Bazhan, Maksym Rylsky, and Ihor Havryluk. For his own poetry, he set the goal of overcoming the narrow political dictates that had long dominated western Ukrainian literature. He also disliked the nativist tonality that manifested itself in an excessive reliance on national folklore in the form of mere stylization. By contrast, when Antonych himself turned to this source, he always did so in order to discover and reach the deepest, archetypical structure of national culture. He strove to restore poetry to its primeval function of providing an intuitive cognition of the universe, taking over the structure of the primeval imagination, he called himself "a pagan in love with life," "a poet of the intoxication of spring."

The second collection, *Three Rings*, which was published in 1934, substantially differs from the first one. It is composed of longer elegies and of short two- or three-stanza miniatures. The thematic nature of each of the two groups is sharply defined: the elegies develop the motif of childhood memories, while in the miniatures the motif of the earth predominates. Moreover, constructed on a powerful single image (or cluster of images), these poems demonstrate a deliberate simplicity of prosody and diction.

In the period of 1935–37, Antonych's interests found artistic expression in a poetic world that reveals characteristics of a sacred transcendental reality. His sensitivity to the irrational aspects of the world found its outlet in the construction of a poetic myth on the one hand—that of Arcadia in primeval times and the concomitant harmony between man and nature. On the other hand he sensed an impending apocalyptic destruction of the world. Thus, Antonych's need for a new poetic idiom was realized in the magical aspects of language, a symbolic type of imagination, and epiphany as the main source of poetic creativity. He breathed vivid life into his poetic images with brilliant musical verse. Moreover, he created a complex figure: the poet as one whose traits unite those of the visionary and those of a craftsman. Antonych's later work wrestles with the philosophical problem of irrational cognition of the world and man's place in it. Here, the central focus of his writing is on a dichotomous view of the universe and nostalgia for an ideal that is both aesthetic and spiritual. The reader of his poetry is continuously confronted with everyday reality versus the distant ideal and with the conception of an endless cycle of existence, with death followed by resurrection, cyclic/sacred time versus linear/historical time, which inevitably brings destruction and the ultimate end of human life.

These concerns explain much about Antonych's isolated position among his fellow Ukrainian writers. Rather than pay homage to the national myth, Antonych aimed to create his own meta-physical myth; rather than content himself with dealing with historical Ukrainian heroes, he went back farther, to the primeval, when man lived in harmony with nature and the universe. Like many European modernists he turned to the primitive and the exotic as the only way of liberating literature from the utilitarian engagement that had prevailed in the Ukrainian tradition and that was still an issue even in the 1930s. In his pursuit of this goal, he avoided overt political commitment of any kind. Antonych's priorities were solely artistic and intellectual, and they acquired religious and metaphysical directions as he increasingly sought to transcend reality to find his "home beyond a star." This distant reality represented for him an imaginative reconstruction of a transcendental level of existence that, in his words, "evokes feelings unattainable in reality." At the same time this was also his own version of the myth of art freed from all restrictions.

Antonych is the poet who introduced the voice of the Other into Ukrainian literature, whose poetic diction was formed by a different experience and heritage from that of most other Ukrainian poets. The specific character of his poetic diction is determined by the poetics of liminality shaped by a larger context of his multicultural heritage. It seems that his rootedness in a bilingual and bicultural environment, as well as his extraordinary talent, helped him to transcend the "aesthetic of struggle" that predetermined the western Ukrainian literary canon of the time and replaced it by his own much more universal artistic paradigm, one that was still "native" yet no longer provincial. Some of his early verse registered the influence of interwar Polish literary groups such as Skamander and the Krakow avant-garde. Antonych's early writings were inspired in particular by two Skamander poets: Julian Tuwim and Kazimierz Wierzyński. Certain aspects of their poetics can be found in Antonych's book *A Welcome to Life*; these appear mainly as an echo of vitalism. The theme of sports in Antonych's poetic cycle "Bronze Muscle" is no doubt an adaptation of Wierzyński's collection *Olympic Laurels* (1928). As for vitalism, and the Dionysian motif in particular, it is manifested first of all as spontaneity and a cult of life perceived as a biological element in Wierzyński's and Tuwim's work from the 1920s. Antonych, to a certain extent, shares with both Polish poets the adoration of life as a goal and the main topic of some of his earliest poems. However, Dionysian motifs in transformed images appear later in *The Book of the Lion* and *The Green Gospel*, where they find a legitimate motivation for building Antonych's own myth of Arcadia and the myth of primeval man. Yet, he never admires technical civilization and the reality of the metropolis, in contrast to early Skamander poetry.

The impact of Walt Whitman, whom Antonych called "a minister of the republic of poets," provides another link between him and Skamander (its members, especially Tuwim, were the first translators of the American poet in Poland). Whitman was the first teacher who discovered for Antonych "the mysteries of the primeval cause" and provided him with an example of poetry that "sings glory to the God-Spirit," through its thousands of "Embodiments of Things," to praise existence and to explain death. But first and foremost, Antonych's mature poetry echoes Whitman's idea of perpetual transformation. It is also arguable that Whitman as a poet of modernity, of the young ideals of democracy and of its unlimited possibilities, might have served as an example in helping Antonych to extract universal features out of the Ukrainian tradition, those that transcend nationalism and the problem of "Ukrainianness"—issues that for a lengthy time were at stake in Ukrainian literature.

Avant-garde tendencies in art provided the second source of inspiration for Antonych. In Poland these were represented best—both in theoretical discourse and poetic practice—by the Krakow avant-garde, a group of writers centered around the poet and theoretician Tadeusz Peiper. In the first instance, avant-garde artistic conceptions influenced Antonych's intense awareness of the literary craft, poetic devices, and the freedom and restrictions of language. Here lie the sources of his interest in metapoetic reflection and his focus on the internal structure of verse. Second, these ideas inspired the antimimetic attitude apparent in his poetic search for more adequate means of expression. Third, similar to Peiper's program, Antonych changed the very conception of the artist—the former model of the poet-prophet (*wieszcz*) is replaced by that of wordsmith (*słowiarz*), a skilled technician who is deeply and consciously aware of his goals and tools. The process of writing is thus compared to craftsmanship, and the poet to the craftsman who consciously reduces his social obligations and aims mainly at building "inventions" in the field of poetic articulation, crafting new linguistic methods intended to surpass previous models of literature. Fourth, these conceptions inspired him to link literature with the methods of the other arts. Thus we can point not only to a strong visual perception, manifested mainly in his mature poetry (some critics classify Antonych as an imaginist), and a powerful musicality, but also to the use of the film techniques of collage and large-plane/small-plane framing. Fifth, conceptualism in Antonych's early writing was not his strongest suit and sounded more like "bookishness;" nevertheless, he was later able to create a much more sophisticated poetic form of this form of expression.

Yet if one turns from the level of literary technique to the world represented in his poetry, one will notice some differences between Antonych's own poetic diction and that of the avant-garde as articulated in Peiper's program. The most significant disfunction is the magico-mythical foundation of Antonych's poetry. This essential difference refers to dissimilar epistemological attitudes: Przyboś (one of the Krakow avant-garde poets), for instance, wanted to state the expressible. Antonych as he sought to give witness to the metaphysical matters of human existence, aimed for the inexpressible. Thus the two poets' respective attitudes toward writing were actually antithetical. Antonych's stance was that of a creator, who summons a world from nothingness by the magical power of the poetic word; Przyboś proceeds like an engineer of language, building his poetic piece from existing materials. Hence, even though we note a strong avant-garde inspiration in Antonych's poetics, the traditions of Romanticism and of Symbolism were of similar importance. The creation of "cosmic" poetry, the search for "the bottom of reality," the quest for the "primeval word" (*praslovo*), the antithetical vision of an ideal reality and everyday life, the constant longing for his mythical "home beyond the star," the poet's rights as creator and prophet, the double-planed vision of reality (the visible and the invisible), the construction of a language and situations imbued with an atmosphere of magic, the awareness of the vagueness and ambiguity of reality, the complex function of musicality—all of this formed a cornerstone of Antonych's poetry after 1935 and indicates a convergence with the poetics of Symbolism, rather than with the avant-garde. However, the term "Symbolism" is used here in a wider sense, referring not to a literary period, but rather to a certain perspective and a way of representing the world that can have an innovative character. This perspective, however, was the characteristic not only for Antonych but also, in Polish literature, for the poetry of the Second avant-garde à la Czesław Miłosz and Józef Czechowicz. Yet the mode of catastrophism predominated in the work of many western European writers of the 1930s and reflected anxiety connected with the rise of fascism, the Spanish Civil War, and the worldwide economic crisis. Antonych was an acute observer of Western literature and this grim atmosphere is echoed in his later poems. For these reasons his later works cannot be ascribed exclusively to Polish inspiration.

Antonych's strong theoretical awareness honed by an avant-garde literary approach can be observed also in the fact that he was the only Ukrainian poet of this period to express his reflections on literature in a systematic way, not only as a poet but also as a theoretician. Metapoetic deliberations appear in many of his articles: "Between Content and Form" (1932), "The Crisis of Contemporary Literature" (1932), "National Art" (1933), "A Hundred Coins of Madness" (1935), "The Stance of the Poet" (1935), and others. The point of departure of his theoretical work was a postulate that Ukrainian literature should break through its traditional aesthetic formed by the experience of Ukrainian Romanticism and continued by the "populists." This was the only chance, he believed, for it to transcend its provincial character as an "ethnographic curiosity," of interest only to a narrow group of enthusiasts. Art, declared Antonych, shall no longer bear any obligation toward the nation—or, at least, not to the nation as it was understood by the populists, who sought to yoke the writer to the politically utilitarian role of a singer who appeals to the patriotic feelings of his countrymen. Even though we do not find a consistent and coherent theoretical system in his articles, Antonych, nevertheless, aimed at an idealistic system of art (as opposed to materialistic theories), and his deep preoccupation with the issues of the poet, poetry, and poetic creativity reflects his struggle to construct his own genuine conception of poetry, whose main function is to explore and comprehend reality, and with this cognition lead us to a transcendence that will enable us to conceive the universe. Thus he formulated his own brief definition of art: "The goal of art is not beauty . . . the goal of art is to elicit in our psyche the kind of experience that real reality does not give us."

Summarizing Antonych's core aesthetic beliefs, one can say that in his view art creates its own reality, art is an autonomous realm of discourse; it reveals a "higher reality," or it gives intuition about aspects of the real world that are inaccessible to rational cognition; it contributes to the process of transforming the real world in the direction of the ideal. As for the poetic work itself, it is seen as the expression of an autonomous human activity, as a verbal act with specific artistic qualities—an assertion that reflects the Symbolist's approach to the cognitive aspect of art. In other words, Antonych insisted that art is not a vehicle of knowledge, but rather an independent form of knowledge, and he shared a belief with the symbolist poets that poetry, is a means of transcending reality. It is true that he did not create his own unified or original theory of poetry, but rather culled certain conceptions of western European Modernism. Nevertheless, he infused those ideas with his own reflections and his awareness of the crisis in Ukrainian literature that led him to look for novel alternatives and to discuss these issues from a theoretical point of view. We can perceive his inclination to neo-Kantian idealistic existentialism (for example in the vein of Rilke and Heidegger) since at the center of Antonych's aesthetic lies not exactly beauty understood as an independent value but rather transcendence, to which beauty refers and which he believed is a "grand harmony"—the absolute truth.

The issue of truth inspired Antonych's poetic search for "the primeval word"; he shared the belief of other Modernists that the primeval word stands at the origins of time and thus bridges the present day with the paradise lost of genuine harmony between man and nature. Thus we are dealing here with poetic activity understood as myth-making; and the myth Antonych creates has ambivalent meaning: on the one hand, there is a vision of Arcadia, where harmony prevails between culture and nature (cyclical time); on the other, a catastrophic vision of present reality (linear time), which Antonych perceives as a time of chaos and the decline of civilization. In his formula of present-versus-past, he clearly regards the past as "better" than the present. His attempt to return to the "better" past, therefore, marks a negation of the contemporary turmoil and chaos that characterized the European reality of the 1930s. Antonych assumed that only through art are we able to integrate this terrible life experience. He believed that poetry provides this opportunity because it enables the poet to attain the primeval word—the word equal to its designate, which implies an elimination of the opposition between the subject and its verbal expression. This effort to reach transcendental reality by means of the poetics of myth found its original poetic articulation in Antonych's volumes *The Book of the Lion* and *The Green Gospel*.

It is evident that the direction of Antonych's thought is close to that of other modernists such as Eliot and Yeats, who investigated the past of language in order to surmount the crisis of culture and the state of human alienation that characterized modern civilization. According to Antonych, this investigation of the linguistic past found its expression in the myth of return, which is supposed to constitute a rediscovery of a nature that is creative and alive. From this standpoint, it seems that the main goal of Antonych's mythmaking, as manifested in his poetic treatment of nature, is to end a state of alienation and the threat to contemporary man, who lives in the state of chaos. At the same time, the possibility of returning to primeval times equals the possibility of animating a dead language.

Antonych's theoretical inclinations naturally directed him toward the metapoetic reflections observed in his literary practice. One of the important elements of that practice is a new form of versification: in contrast to the previous model (the poem divided into verses), meter and intonation now become primary categories in organizing the structure of a work. Although extreme formal experimentation with verse was not of particular interest to Antonych, in his later works, although using traditional stanzas, he introduces certain innovations such as a monumental seven- or eight-foot iambic line (for which he was criticized by most of the literati of his time, particularly by Sviatoslav Hordynsky).

In his poetic practice Antonych also introduces a different kind of reception: the notion of arrangement from the writer's perspective was related to the idea of re-arrangement from the perspective of the reader. The issue of the new Ukrainian implied reader was extremely important in this period. In challenging the ossified western Ukrainian canon of writing, Antonych challenged the implied reader inherited as part of this canon. And, as he himself predicted, although in general his poetry was praised, his works were, nevertheless, widely misread. He was criticized above all for incomprehensibility. The difficulty and complexity of the task of opening Ukrainian poetry to new sources of inspiration is evident from the complicated reception of Antonych's literary works, not only by his readers but also by the critics and literary scholars of this period. For example, Malaniuk and Rudnytsky complimented Antonych only for his first two books, whose overall tone is in the traditional Ukrainian canon, but criticized his later works, which introduce a new poetics; they blamed him for "pointless experimentation."

Besides a new form of versification and a new implied reader, Antonych was concerned particularly with two other essential avant-garde premises. First, there is the conception of the poet-craftsman, who single-handedly creates a world: in *The Book of the Lion* and *The Green Gospel*, he often uses the metaphor of a craftsman of the word (*teslia slova/remisnyk slova*). This outlook demonstrates that Antonych continues Plato's dual definition of the poet as both a seer and a maker; despite his frequent reference to the poetic imagination, his writing also contains numerous appeals for recognition of the poet's work as a skilled craft. Hence, besides poetry conceived as a product of outside revelation and inspiration (vision), in Antonych's oeuvre we also find the conception of the meticulous "maker." His second concern is the notion of the "construction" of a poem and the selection of images and attempts to escape from the "theme-event" unity of sequence that was obligatory in the traditional model of poetry. The selection of subject matter indicated concentrated attention to the composition of a single poem as well as an entire book of poetry. He first introduced this innovative characteristic as a theoretician in the article "National Art," but it played an extremely important role in his literary practice—in his third and fourth collections he introduced a twofold formal division of works, grouping the longer poems into "chapters" and the shorter works into "intermezzos," which differ also in terms of theme and mode. In brief, Antonych's poetic quest for a synthesis of vision and construction, not only at the level of image and inner structure of the text, but of the mythical versus the rational comprehension of reality, lies at the cornerstone of his poetics.

It is in the theory of metaphor, however, that we notice the closest similarities between Antonych's poetics and that of the avant-garde. According to the definition given by Peiper, to use a metaphorical construction is to build, in a lyrical utterance, a new state of things. The prominent Ukrainian critic Orest Zilyns'kyi correctly noted that, "There is an essential difference between Antonych's metaphor and that of the greater part of other Ukrainian poets. For them a metaphor emphasizes a realistic image as a musical chord does. In Antonych's metaphor, however, it becomes a building block of the entire poetic fiction of his imaginative world, in which things intertwine into new functional clusters. And this is, properly speaking, already not a metaphor, but an organic part of a new separate reality." (Zilyns'kyi 99) Zilyns'kyi's observation is very accurate—in Antonych's metaphor, particularly beginning with *The Book of the Lion*, we observe a distortion of the relationships among objects, and this becomes a tool with which to build a different reality. In his longer poems written after 1935, he composes monumental sequences of images that he reinvigorates by focusing on a visionary mode of expression (often surreal) with painterly imagery and musical effects, by uniquely constructing metaphors to make them visually and aurally striking, by applying a technique of film-like montage of sequences of different images, and by creating unexpected juxtapositions of vocabulary and imagery drawn from various semantic areas.

Although Antonych was brought up in Poland and steeped in Polish culture as a native speaker, he never wrote anything in Polish. He read Polish literature but did not identify himself with it. Antonych, however, strove to break away from a populist understanding of nationality, which, for a long time, demanded that the artist be "national"—which in practice meant to serve the needs of the nation in its attempt to maintain a patriotic spirit. Thus in the populists' eyes, a real national art employed national symbols and imagery and referred to historical events and folk motifs. Antonych disagreed with this opinion and addressed it in the article "National Art: An Attempt at an Idealistic System of Art":

It is important to remember the truth that is already known and has been expressed many times, but is still not accepted and widespread—that national character in art is not created by themes of national folklore or history, nor by the imitation of folklore or our old ways of formulating a work of art. It is a shame to repeat such a commonplace, but I must. . . . The artist is "national" when he identifies himself with a certain nation and feels the concordance of this psyche with the collective psychology of his nation. If this feeling is honest, it will certainly find an expression—even involuntary—in the artist's work. (Antonych 469)

"National Art" is Antonych's most substantial theoretical work and the most direct expression of his different comprehension of what national art means. It was published in *Karby*, a collection of articles on the art of the Association of Ukrainian Independent

Artists. It is interesting that the members of AUIA were exclusively avant-garde painters and sculptors; Antonych was the first writer accepted into the organization: after the publication of his article they acknowledged him as their theoretician. Why? What did it mean to be an "independent Ukrainian artist" at the time? It seems that the main reason for his acceptance was that Antonych aimed at challenging a "petrified" national style, and he was consciously using his Polish heritage to help him do so. Regarded from this standpoint, Polish literature, at least at the outset of his work, provided him with ready patterns absent in Ukrainian literature. At the same time, a "contact situation" (Uriel Weinreich's term), complicated by his experience of liminality in both cultures, demanded from him self-determination not only as a Ukrainian, but primarily as an artist. He found himself on the border of the two cultures, and he therefore functioned as a kind of mediator between the different traditions. The Ukrainian literary language was, in a sense, much like a foreign language for him, and he had to study intensively to master it; this struggle with language became a unique experience for the talented poet who was able to use it as a positive value and a factor that shaped his poetic diction. However, as noted above, Ukrainian scholars, although they acknowledge Antonych's Lemko origins, have consistently overlooked the aesthetic implications of his multicultural and bilingual roots, particularly as manifested in his early works. In *A Welcome to Life* we can identify many linguistic mistakes in his use of normative literary Ukrainian (in subsequent books Antonych makes fewer and fewer errors), demonstrating that at the beginning of his literary activity he was not in complete command of his literary Ukrainian.

Critics have still not yet completely acknowledged Antonych's importance in the evolution of Ukrainian poetry. They still hesitate in assigning him a specific place on the spectrum of twentieth-century Ukrainian literature. Although he himself associated his poetry with that of the avant-garde, he construed it as a general trend of contemporary poetry rather than as a specific poetics. Notwithstanding particular schools and literary movements, Antonych spoke of an "avant-garde attitude," which he identified with a constant search for new and more adequate expression, a constant creativity, a constant becoming and elaboration on artistic cognitive power. However, this creative instability was essentially post-Romantic.

Another reason for the difficulty in fitting Antonych into a narrow classification scheme is that he was able to write in differing, even opposing, modes. He began as a romantic rebel in *A Welcome to Life*, regressed to dreams and the experience of childhood in *Three Rings*, and finally reinvented himself as a visionary and mythmaker, whose diction might be expressed as something on the edge of Symbolist and avant-garde poetry, but which cannot be easily described by the critics. Antonych's ability to make use of different modes of expression and different perspectives, and his openness to the polyphony of voices and forms, reveals his belief that the best way to recognize and grasp the unity of being is by demonstrating the continuous *coincidentia oppositorum* that characterize our earthly world of time and space. In the higher, transcendental reality "beyond the star," however, these oppositions are surpassed, and can be recognized as part of a unity, the eternal wholeness that is intuitively sensed by the artist. To be able to express these reflections Antonych had to find his own poetic idiom. He did so by surpassing both of the aesthetics that shaped the core of his poetry: Symbolism and the avant-garde. Antonych shared with Symbolism a nostalgia for a "higher world," a type of imagination, and the musical structure of his verse; with the avant-garde he shared a respect for poetic craft, and the aspects of rigor, indirectness, and tight construction. Yet he was far from someone who reduced poetry to mere poetic craft since he conceived of it as a metaphysical quest.

The importance of Antonych in Ukrainian poetry of the twentieth century cannot be overestimated. He introduced an innovative mode of expression and did so on multiple levels: that of archetypal imagery and metaphysics (even mysticism), indicative of his search for eternity; a contemplation of the essence of things; and a masterful craftsmanship. All these were instrumental in converting western Ukrainian poetry from something exhausted by realism and monotonized by political dictates into a freer, more imaginative poetic tonality. As a modernist, he emphasized the self-referential aspect of literature. His entire life was immersed in art, which (like Wallace Stevens, for example) he saw as an everyday necessity: "daily bread" in his words. Moreover, Antonych used his familiarity with contemporary western European artistic tendencies and theories in an effort to reawaken interest in the theory of literature and metapoetic considerations in western Ukraine. As is evident from his manuscripts, he highly valued Paul Valéry (in the first instance his essays *Sur la technique littéraire*, 1889, and *Les Droits du poète sur la langue*, 1928). Like Valéry, he advocated the study of poetic creation, independent of historical and critical factors. The self-reflective, hyper-conscious aspects of Symbolism were at the center of his interests. Rather than following the Romantic idea of poetry as primary expression of the human spirit, Valéry described poetry as a "constructive science" of precise verbal combinations and "byproduct." Similarly, in his theoretical writing, Antonych emphasizes not only inspiration and epiphany as the only possible sources of art, but also the rational aspect of poetic craft. This was a way to establish the relationship in poetry between the work of the irrational and the rational mind. Antonych's entire oeuvre manifests this poetic span between vision and construction.

The high intrinsic value of his art along with his bridging of avant-garde ideas and the poetry of myth make Antonych a focal point of twentieth-century Ukrainian poetry. His work signified that Ukrainian poetry was entering a new stage—a philosophical rather than a political one. In his attempt to create a universal vision of the world, the relation between poet, society, and nation is weakened—or, at least, it becomes much less important than it had been in the prevailing canon of Ukrainian literature of the time. Antonych reaches his own, original poetic diction by sharpening the epistemological issues of literature, something that is emphasized by his innovative poetic devices.

Finally, we come to the fundamental issue: how to conceptualize Antonych's conversion from marginality to centrality. How did he shape his own poetic form of expression from heteroglossia? The answer is complex. Certainly, a decentering of his Polish heritage played an extremely important role. The experience of cultural liminality seems to have been much stronger for Antonych than for his colleagues because Ukrainian itself was an acquired language for him. One can argue that his struggle toward mastering it was more than simply a manifestation of "language loyalty"; it also gave him the experience of a different perception, a different way of hearing sounds and intonation—an experience that is undergone by everyone who studies and absorbs a new language. His "struggle" with the Ukrainian literary language was therefore also a method of facilitating his quest for his own authentic and fresh poetic voice. Over time writing exclusively in Ukrainian (initially, in his early writings, by adapting Polish poetic models) helped him, on the one hand, to achieve a certain distance from the subject matter and structure of Polish poetry, and, on the other, to grasp the new tonality and possibilities for artistic expression contained in Ukrainian. In this sense, his decentering of his Polish cultural heritage also served as a strategy of liberation, a way of freeing himself from a "strong" tradition (in Harold Bloom's sense of the word), not so much as a Ukrainian as simply a poet.

From this standpoint, Antonych's innovative poetic diction can be viewed as the voice of the "other" since the ontological status of his poetics is created by the situation and experience of growing up in a bilingual environment, and thus in a liminal cultural environment. One of the purposes of Antonych's "poetic revolution" was to regain an independent cultural position, to successfully reinsert Ukrainian culture into the European mainstream. If the bulk of Ukrainian poetry of the time consisted of reactions against Polish and Russian political and cultural domination, this marked not only an awakened national consciousness, which was part of the general atmosphere of the time, but was also symptomatic of a crisis of identity and an inferiority complex. For this reason, Antonych consciously rejected what he perceived as the perpetually backward-looking tradition associated with the Ukrainian "populists." In his poetry he tried to exploit his natural inclination toward the larger context of European art and to write in a mode other than that of ideology. His efforts in this area were not exceptional in this part of Europe. The Polish literature of the period had been dealing with similar problems: after it regained its freedom in 1918, many young writers launched an attack on the old literary canon, and the most active among them were the poets from groups such as Skamander and the Krakow avant-garde. Antonych's liminal position, therefore, seems to have been the main impetus that propelled the process by which he shaped his original poetics. No wonder one of the most important issues of his poetry is the issue of identity—not a national identity, but an artistic one. It seems probable that the search for artistic identity became a reason and a source for Antonych's frequent reflections on issues of metapoetics.

The issue of liminality was not, however, the only factor in this process. The complexity of the conversion of Antonych's poetic voice reveals itself also in how he sought to create a universal vision of the world by which modern times could be grasped. Thus an attempt to explain this phenomenon exclusively as a "struggle for the new aesthetics" does not exhaust our inquiry. For Antonych it was ultimately an attempt to find an answer to the question of what we should do, how we can live in a contemporary world that has drastically lost its hierarchy of values through the scientific and relativistic Weltanschauung (concerns radically presented by Nietzsche). As we know, this was also the central issue for other modernists such as Eliot and Rilke and in Poland, Czechowicz and Miłosz. Thus the central focus for these poets was the comprehension of art as an act that creates the values that put order into chaos, or, essentially the same thing, an act that creates God, that is, a substitute for religion. ("Poetry is a secular type of religion," Marko utters in Antonych's unfinished novel, "On the Other Shore") (*Na druhomu berezi*). In the 1930s, the time when Antonych was writing, a time when premonitions of war hung heavy in the air, this issue gained even greater importance. Here we find the source of Antonych's catastrophic visions of the city and the time in which he lived. Like the modernist poets mentioned above, he felt that it was impossible for the human imagination to shape space and time in a religious way and that this impossibility has its equivalent in the chaos and disintegration of interhuman relations in the modern world. This perception and sensibility of Antonych is demonstrated in the "Second Chapter" of *The Book of the Lion* and in the book *Rotations*, in the images of fragmentation and decay.

In sum, we can assert that Antonych is undoubtedly one of the most important poets of Ukrainian literature in the twentieth century. For a long time he was not published in Soviet Ukraine; only in 1967 was a collection of his poetry edited and published by Dmytro Pavlychko under the title *A Song on the Indestructibility of Matter* (*Pisnia pro neznyshchennist' materii*). It is significant that his work was embraced with enthusiasm not only by the Ukrainian Writers of the Sixties generation, but also by the Ukrainian writers who debuted during perestroika, and who precisely stated their anti-political resonance in order to focus on the aesthetic values of art. In this sense, Antonych is their direct intellectual predecessor. Paradoxically, he still has become a "national poet," although not through political involvement, but rather through his transcendence over Ukrainian provincialism. For these reasons, from today's vantage point, Antonych's role and importance in Ukrainian literature can be compared to that of Yeats in Irish literature since Antonych did something similar for Ukrainian literature: like Yeats, he moved the literature toward metaphysics and philosophy by "stimulat[ing] a sense of the eternal." His goal of reevaluating the role of art in a Ukrainian context was a clear challenge to the existing Ukrainian literary canon, the bulk of whose literature constituted a reaction against the impact of Polish and Russian political and cultural domination. The purpose of his "poetic revolution" was to transcend cultural isolation and to find a way of regaining an independent cultural position and of successfully reinserting a distinctively Ukrainian culture into the European mainstream. Antonych aimed at providing a new model of literature, something other than the limited and limiting vision of the nativist. He sought to rise above national interests, in the name of universal values, so that a national myth could be connected with a myth of eternity. As noted by Edward Said, the colonial perspective makes us realize that despite the tremendous, resentful emotional power that often accompanies nativism, it must be refused because it leads to an impasse. To accept nativism is to accept the consequences of colonial subordination. The new alternative to nativism, as Said suggests, "is liberation: a transformation of social consciousness beyond national consciousness" (Said 227). From the perspective of liberation, Yeats's slide into incoherence and mysticism, his rejection of politics, his insistence on a new narrative for his people, is much the same as other poets resisting imperialism. It is a kind of surreptitious counternarrative. Antonych's poetry in this sense was also, in a Ukrainian setting, a counternarrative. Its significance lies in its ability, while marginalized by Polish and Russian cultures, to reverse the reductive and slanderous encapsulation of Ukrainian actualities. Antonych must be thought of as a Ukrainian poet with a more-than-strictly-local meaning and application. The power of his accomplishment is that he restored the human need, suppressed by centuries of colonization, for metaphysical, non-political meditation on the meaning of life, eternity and art, purely for their own sakes (rather than in the name of national interests, where literature had to play a didactic role designed to amplify the patriotic feelings of the reader). Thus Antonych rises from the level of personal experience to that of universal archetype.

Works Cited

Antonych, Bohdan Ihor. 1998. "Natsional'ne mystetstvo." In *Bohdan Ihor Antonych: Tvory*, 467–76. Kyiv: Vydavnytstvo khudozhn'oi literatury.

Said, Edward. 1993. "Yeats and Decolonization." In *Culture and Imperialism*, 220–38. New York: Vintage Books.

Zilyns'kyi, Orest. 1989. "Dim za zoreiu." In *Vesny rozspivanoi kniaz': Slovo pro Antonycha*, 87–119. Lviv: Kamieniar.

The Essential Poetry of
Bohdan Ihor Antonych

PART I

From the Collection
The Grand Harmony (1932–1933)

Music of the Night

Light up the torch of the pale moon in the sky,
illuminate the darkness of the night with stars,
let hearts that are sick with loneliness take comfort
when they see thousands of Your worlds.

In a heart wrapped in the scarves of quiet peace,
melodious, harmonious is every tone.
The distance echoes with just barely audible harps,
wind tunes the night by the tuning fork of God.

Like beautiful, full-grown summer on spring's flood,
a ripe fullness has matured in your soul.
Slightly darkened gray colors, just on the horizon
in the distance, the golden cupola of the setting sun.

The warm summer night rises in the fragrances of many flowers
high on mountain crests and wooded peaks.
Let us listen to the great concert in the evening as
God places his hands on the piano of the world.

March 23, 1932

On Death I

I will bow my head in thought only later
above the river of life that has passed
and gaze in mute, quiet sorrow
at the riverbed covered with silt.

Only later, perhaps, in forty years or so,
when I am a miserable man, expressionless,
will I shake life's dust
from my torn pilgrim's vestments.

Only later, perhaps, in forty years or so,
an average person of no note,
will I see truth through the gloom
and cast aside my pilgrim's staff.

An angel will appear and write
the judgment on azure paper with his sword,
death will come and with a silver key
unlock the door of eternity for me.

March 23, 1932

I am an ordinary poet,
each day fascinates me.
I do not understand the world,
I do not understand my own songs.

To drink ecstasy to the brim . . .
A carefree voice like a cricket,
this is the way I sing,
just an echo still ringing in the mountains.

The beginning of rapture,
of religion and sonnets;
rapture gives birth to our
apostles and poets.

I do not know how to write poems,
I scoff at the rules and standards.
For me it is God Himself
who forms my poetics.

Thursday, March 24, 1932

Book of Pilgrims 3 (Jerusalem)

The yellow road beneath my feet,
the blue sky above us.
I walk along unknown paths.
Man is an eternal pilgrim . . .

I miss laughter and spring,
the birds are singing above me,
ringing songs soar in a din
before this mute pilgrim.

I carry my burden on my shoulders,
the gift of God in a blue box,
though the fierce heat of the swelter burns,
though the vicious wind whips.

And so I wander without stopping
I push along every day like rosary beads,
and I will rest only
when I reach Jerusalem.

Sunday, March 27, 1932

PART II

From the Collection
*Three Rings: Long Poems
and Lyrics* (1934)

SELF-PORTRAIT

Red and silver maples,
Spring and the wind above them.
The incomprehensible beauty of nascence,
is it possible not to get high from you?

Having sold life to the sun
for a hundred gold coins of madness,
I am forever an ecstatic pagan,
a poet of the high of spring.

On the wall a winged violin,
a black jug, a flowery box.
Creative fires slumber in the violin,
the musical dew is silver and deep blue.

In the flowery box a singing root,
an intoxicating herb, wax, and seeds,
and at the very bottom three stars,
the bright stone of three rings.

In the crimson jug a mint libation,
green maple droplets.
Bells, a winged string,
for love and mad spring!

The top is being lifted up,
the jug is circling, the box singing.
And the sun, like a flaming bird,
and morning, leaning against a fence.

AN ELEGY ABOUT A SINGING DOOR

A singing door, a gray maple,
an old painted doorstep.
This is the way places of my childhood days
have remained in my imagination,
this way the memory of a boy has preserved
the already darkened images,
the scope of that quivering song
became so confined
that it emotionally stirs
and without an excess tear
paints landscapes of recollections.
And once again I want to experience
a boy's joys and storms . . .
Blood courses quicker through veins
and sullen eyes shine with happiness,
a quill pen becomes light in your palm.

On mountaintops gray grass,
dark red stones in the river.
Tar-black night, and a swarthy day,
like a gypsy woman's face.
Impassioned laughing streams,
like lovers to girls, flutter to deep valleys
that sleep quietly in gray gloom,
and the scent of flowers wafts,
like smoke from colorful pipes.
Firs quiver in the paws of the wind,
lament in a slight whisper,
droplets of froth flow down,
like tar from hot stumps.
Wrapped in green and pensiveness,
a deer drinks water from a spring.
The flowery sun sleeps in the well

on the moss-covered bottom.
As a burning bush of mystery
it comes out from the depth in the morning.
A thicket sings in a shaggy dream,
it began to hum in an ancient rustle.
On the slope of mountains like patches
the village is sewn into the forest.

The country tavern, like a bush that gives birth to stars,
is lit with candles in the night.
Translucent vapor rises from the liquor,[1]
rusty keys scrape.
Gypsies cut a rug with a fiery bow,
the bass is singing deep and fast.
The musician is cooking, and the voice is dark,
and the fierce rattle of drunken strings.
Ten fingers quiver on a flute,
the musical wood is burning.
From a tambourine as though from a jug
a doubled hot scream pours out.
The fiddle burns, grows quiet, withers,
the heart of the tambourine drunk with song.
The bass tells us about the *opryshky*[2] for the upteenth time:
sacred orbs, a solid belt,
a mysterious herb, a wild hive in a stump,
a damned night and death in libations
the devil brews for lovers.
A mad moon—a fanciful tenor
leads the mystical song of darkness.
A girl, like a spindle,
rustles her skirts in a dance.

1 The Ukrainian word for vodka, which comes from the verb *hority* (to burn).
2 Rebels who revolted against the rule of the Polish and Ukrainian nobility in the
sixteenth and seventeenth centuries in the Carpathian Mountains.

I still remember: the morning sows
quivering sparks on the water.
I still remember: a white house
where walls are made of wood and a dream.
I still remember: in the sun
a bridge lazily warms a red back
like a giant cat
that screws up its eyes in lazy sleep.
And the house and bridge, perhaps, are still standing,
but for me have already passed
and burn just in memory.
An insatiable raven cawed above the bridge,
the sun flowed like a river to the world.
I used to go there to catch crayfish
when I was five.
The wild rose pricked my tiny fingers,
with my lips I sucked the sweet blood.
The little boy gazed at the stars
but didn't find his own.

Here troubled people have
a gray sky and gray eyes.
Rainy weather resounds and wets the blinds,
carries on hushed conversations.
Beneath the gray sky the land
of oats and juniper spreads out.
Sadness has wrapped
this pensive land in moss.
As a symbol of misery
a ravenous herb grows—pigweed.
The sky is sempiternal and boundless,
the eternal Lemko need.

Ancient goddess Lada[3] in the mysterious precipices
tells fortunes for young boys.
Christ's incense burns in the churches,
and the smoke of prayer smolders.
In the sky only blue stars
listen to the entreating song of the people
who, simple and wingless,
in mute submission kissing
the dirty legs of altars
with their mouths, black from the dust
that covers their lips,
they send their prayers to Christ and the Spirit
to help them acquire money
for bread, salt and their liquor.

The earth bears no fruit, the wind blows,
moss is on the field like warm clothing,
but people, as in this world,
keep being born, suffer, and die.
Fires and downpours pass,
leaving just wastelands,
wars rumble and pass,
rulers change,
the years flow like mountain water,
and the autumn rain just generates
recollections about the *opryshky*.
Many storms have blown over.
You alone are the same never changing
far-off Lemko village.

I send words there like arrows,
a winged song rushes in that direction.
I came from just such a village,

3 The Slavic goddess of spring and love.

a celebrator of life—a highlander.
From people who are sincere and the everyday kind,
who have peacefully accepted their ration of fate,
and who have knelt down to the mystery of the heavens
under the sign of the singing crescent.
And, perhaps, I would have remained here
like others, I would have submitted,
and, having fallen down to the earth mute,
I would have prayed to the joyous oats,
but He, who gave lightness of foot to the doe,
and golden flowers to the bees,
and steel claws to the lynx,
gave singing words to me
and sharp teeth, so that in life
I could firmly and simply defend myself.

The wide world, wider than the heart
and a wider wind in the village.
In this poem I can't fit
the stars, the sky, or the earth.
Wide paths into immense space.
I went into the world as a boy.
In truth time does not halt,
though it is difficult for us to understand.
Anxieties, joys, deceptions,
love, betrayal, dark nights,
and a gray-eyed girl.
The madness of despair, and love's ardor,
the intoxication of happiness and sorrow,
the frenetic rapture of prayer,
the deep corrosive nature of apathy
and the highest grace of creativity—
life has given all of this to me.
I extol it here
and call to the days: make me intoxicated,
intoxicate me! Though death be closer,

though there is rust on the past,
though the first snow disappears,
thoughts ceaselessly quiver,
and each, like crystal, is clear.
O, youth, you alone
are not stained and are good.

The singing azure, a branchy pine,
and a hewn, ringing threshold.
This is the way imagination paints
the places of a boy's dreams and delights.

I.

A green leaf, a winged key,
a spindle and a ring,
and the intoxicating cabal of youth
again gets you drunk as it once used to.
To burn again and freeze again,
to love again and get high again!
On your finger is an elegiac ring,
and elegiac April on your heart.

The white town is in a night glow.
Shouldn't I mention my friends here?
We grew up together and used to get high
from loving passionate girls.
We hid from restless daydreams,
we imitated the proud and firm
and tore into the boundless expanses
that spread at our feet.
Bright youth filled with gifts
like a chest filled with treasures,
and a dram—the dark flower of night—
led us, where the boundary of horizons
allured like a song of love.
The blade on knives grew notched,
impulses grew enflamed.
Houses bedecked by the moon,
and trembling we loved
though we felt embarrassed by love.

It happened this way: like a hot tulip
the sun burned for youthful dreams.
Spring turned to melody

chimed to a hundred pianos.
She curved fiddlesticks into bows
and transformed spindles,
she bawled in a hundred fiddles,
she took drink in mint wells,
spread out in a flowery sackcloth
and strewed out songs and sand.

You remember: spring was aflame
like a girl in love.
You timidly stepped out from the opposite direction
to meet incomprehensible happiness.
You remember: a gypsy wind
stole kisses from the girls.
It emblazoned four hot letters of love
on your heart.
We met. Spring buzzed
like an arrow that cuts the sky.
A girl, drunken with fire,
loved and withered from love.

A letter carrier was carrying green leaves,
the leaves rustled. Hey, spring!
I weave songs on a spindle
about youth that is passing.

II.

An ocarina played in the nights,
blacksmiths sang in a bass voice.
A timid and passionate boy
couldn't find words of love.
White carpenters sang in the morning,
the home of the weavers whirled in a circle.
The boy traced a map of love,
the twelve rings of spring.

This is the way song was born in the heart,
everything turned into song.
The moon leaned on the embrasure
and along the pane, like a droplet, it floated off.
Gazing into lips that call,
into the fire of laughter-filled tears,
you have sculpted in memory a face
to pour it into song.
You loved and betrayed your love,
but you didn't betray your song.
You've always been faithful to it, you walked
into dark midnight to search for words in the forest.

This is the way that life and song have intertwined,
flowing into one.
The despair of inspiration and late joy,
where do the words lead me?
The avid heart of a young boy
experienced love and despair this way.
For greedy lips there are always too few
ardent kisses. So it
stopped trembling, shivered,
glimmered, and ceased to echo,
and flashed and withered,
turned into a painful song.

Like a potter of strophes who molds jugs
from the sung clay of words,
changing lament and laughter
into a lyrical craft and merchantry,
with a persistent heart I have understood
that two things are best of all:
pure love and
                somber
                        art.
White carpenters sang in the morning,

the laughter of weavers on spindles.
A boy traced scorching strophes,
twelve rings of spring.
A letter carrier was carrying green leaves,
the leaves rustled. Hey, spring!
I weave songs on a spindle
about youth that is passing.

Spring springs are singing,
red rings are chiming,
and the intoxicating cabal of youth
again blazes as it once used to blaze.

I have a house, and a garden,
with lyrical apple trees in it.
Like fresh milk, the dew,
the honey of diversion for a spirited me.
Like a hat, a flowery roof,
and a house painted like a treasure chest.
Bandits walk through the gardens
through the hedges and the fences.
It definitely needs to be fenced,
with a wall made of stone and a dream.
The sun grows in my garden—
the intoxicating bloom of tobacco.

I enter the garden and
I give wings
to my young, troubled and persistent heart
with the green scherzo of a sadly singing cherry tree.
I enter the garden as the sun goes down
and the evening, like a string, quivers.
To experience life beguiling
and beautiful in a single minute!
I enter the garden, I pluck words,
the bountiful tribute of inspired trees.
Oh, young boy, you in despair
gaze into the eyes of frenetic beauty!

The elegiac evening has burned out,
it has faded like a song, turned to ashes.
Gather your peaceful words into a wooden jug,
your prayerfully youthful song!
Like a campfire the sun has burned down,
it has burned my eyes with the blaze.

In a burning garland I timidly
bow my joyful brow.

It grew dark. It grew smoky,
the night smokes like a hundred censers.
The sun has rolled into a circle
to meet the moon and the darkness.
Blossoming smoke, a dark blue gloom,
sew the night on the sky with stars.
You, young boy, be careful,
the night will corrode your eyes with the dew.

Again the gust of the lily of the valley is fragrant,
blood saturated with honey.
Though your step is peaceful measured out,
an inconsolable heart beats once again.
Master of the garden—a youthful lyric poet,
I slowly walk to the song of the night.
In my overburdened hand I carry
a basket filled with ripe moons.

The trees rustle mournfully.
Of what do they rustle?
                              —Love and dreams.
The stifling embraces of evenings
will rock the heart into its captivity this way.
Mysterious shadows—flowers of the night
are souls of whitewashed trees.
They want to fly to the moon,
but the wind will not take them away.

O, sorrow grand and joyful,
arrowy words into the heavens!
This is the moon—a young musician
is tuning the garden like a violin.
Uncontrolled and imaginary reverie!

The path of the night spread out into the unknown.
No, the sky will not return those words,
nor will the earth.

Listen to the trees! Write down
their confession in the book of the night!
Like a sycamore catching its own shadow,
stoop to your own soul!
In the book of the night silver letters,
inspired pages rustle.
You will not take it in your hands,
you need to take it to your heart.
Like stars sleeping in the depth,
illuminated by an imaginary dream,
words on the bottom of your winged soul
will awaken and
the bottom answers in song.
The sycamore answers in song,
the night answers in song,
an inconsolable footstep stops.
With the inspired compass of imagination
you will outline a circle of equal strophes.

Let your intoxicated heart at that moment
become winged and burn,
let your troubled and winged thoughts
fly up and break loose
into the heights!
O, word, that quivers in my lips,
must I really stop you?
I feel you approach, black,
intoxicating and melancholy song,
the sharp form seeks content,
the only one for which my horror will have room
and my bright joy
and the entire depth of my exhaustion

and I simply cut into my heart with a word
until blood bursts, like a shout of despair,
with delirium and from happiness I am dying.

On the door of the house is an evil sign,
on the door of the house—is the ring of a song.

THE WEDDING

It began like this: I became intoxicated
from my own first strophes of drunkenness.
Only the moon was best man
at my wedding to a song.
How this happened, how it all began to ring,
I wouldn't know how to tell you,
if only my heart were not burning so.
The first iambs were born this way.
Words not forged in a foundry,
words silver-plated in fire.
Joyful songs are typeset
in the flowering print shop of spring.

An old tale tells of
young girls and merchants.
A goblet with wings in your hand,
thirst and the brew condenses in your blood.

Gold coins clang on the table,
and the moon is a most intoxicating goblet.
The evening bends over to the earth
and spreads out the river in a silver glow.

Toss a song to the wind,
words to the wind!
Somewhere branches whispering,
somewhere grass stirring.

You swim not into deep water,
but into the sun.
Think, really great:
this world is without bounds!

The wind blows a young life
into sprouting seeds,
places hands on
the strings of an apple tree.

There are no apples yet . . .
Someone calls from the ravines.
Listen: this is a finch,
your gray friend.

You're sleepy awake,
you're drunken from dreams.
Somewhere the sycamore
in a whisper welcomes spring.

Somewhere the plum trees are stirring . . .
What more do you want?
Today you're a happy bird,
indeed!

Look: a fine day is churning,
a green blizzard is seething.
It is cooking hollyhock in a thick wooden jug,
so much so that the foam is splashing all the way from there.

A rain of cinnabar resounds along the windowpanes
and the glass sparkles like steel.
The skyline steams in dust,
stirring in the haze of morning salvos.

Raising your eyes from a book,
you will see the world in a colorful dream
and a thought, torn out furtively,
beats at the window like a moth.

A green ash tree, a crescent and horses.
A boy pressed up to the window.
Spring poured into
silver and red goblets.

And the little boy desperately wants
the key to the vernal gates.
The sun unexpectedly jumps out of the grass,
like a frightened colt.

A PRINCE

Mountains are still smoking from the snow,
seven arrows, like seven songs
and the day greets a young lad
with a winged name: Ihor.

Fiddles burn in the wedding gate,
on it the multihued flag of the day.
I walk in delight and ecstasy,
the prince of many-voiced spring.

MAPLES

Two lonely maples bent down
to read the primer of spring
            again I pray to the green earth
            I am young myself like the grass.

A learned fox overgrown with moss
has created a poetics for the maples.
            The day sings, the maples sing,
            a sunny arrow jabbers.

Cows pray to the sun
that rises like a fiery poppy.
A slender poplar gets thinner and thinner,
as if the tree might become a bird.

The moon is untied from the wagon.
An expansive hempen sky.
The endless distance is wind-filled,
and in the gray haze of the forest a crest.

From the mountains sycamore leaves gush.
Flax, a rooster, and a cradle.
The day pours into the dale,
Like fresh milk into a bowl.

God was born on a sleigh
in the Lemko village of Dukli.
The Lemkos arrived in their wide-brimmed hats
they brought a round moon.

The night circles around
thatched roofs in a snowstorm.
Mary has the moon—a golden hazelnut—
in the palm of her hand.

KOLYADA[1]

Carpenters hew a sled from silver,
the snowy path spreads out.
They will carry off the child of God
into the unknown blue on those sleds.

Carpenters hew a sled of silver,
they dream springtime dreams.
On that sled is the Bright Lady,
with eyes like a doe.

The sun is walking in a wide-brimmed hat,
the Slavic Child is sleeping.
The sled moves, the Lady weeps,
life spreads out in the snow.

1 Kolyada is the name of an ancient Slavic god of the winter solstice, later adopted
as the name for Ukrainian Christmas carols (*kolyadky*) that singers (*kolyadnyky*) sing
moving from house to house.

Spring is like a carousel,
on the carousel white horses.
A mountain village in gardens of apricots
and the sun, like a tulip, red.

A table made of ash, on the table
a Slavic wooden jug, in the jug the sun.
You should worship just the earth,
the multihued earth, like this dream!

I.

We sail out into a sea of pines,
into the rustle of pines, a pine song . . .
Above us is the boundless sky,
above us a roof of slender treetops,
above us oily stumps steam
with a deep breath.

And you sense fragrant herbs growing
beneath your footsteps.

Here we desire nothing else—
but to cover ourselves in the moss of dreams,
in the ancient primeval darkness of nature,
to fall into the primordial depth.

Let a thick resin seethe
in our body, as though in pine trees.
Let the faint greenery and flame
as well as the azure flow into our veins.

II.

We will grow into the earth like pines
(unfurling banners of the forest).
The languid juice of plants—green blood—
will flow into our veins.

Legs will root into the clay,
hands will become overgrown in leaves.
And bees will rush to your eyes.
And they will drink the honey as though from flowers . . .

It is already not blood—a heavy oil
in hardened kernels bloats,
like raspberries the reverie ripens,
sweet, passionate, and intoxicating.

By the road you will grow
as a red bush in the rustle of silence.
Just a deer—

                    a slender-legged stag
looking for a timid doe.

A snake plantlike and bushy,
a snake sinuous and slimy,
like a wet checkered cane,
sings in the hands of a boy.

A tufted snake, like a hollyhock,
grows from beneath a stone as a bush.
Words plantlike and wavelike
fly down in a joyful rain.

Like a fern, before your eyes
Your ancient primordiality rises.
You still are a plant, you still are a stone,
the snake coils around you.

Learn the language of the forest
from the book of foxes and deer!
The moon comes out to the oak grove
to write elegies on stumps.

Streams sprinkle the silver of silence,
grass bathes in dew.
Let night write the simplest of words
in the book of the forest!

Becoming high on the toxic fumes
of nights bitter and silver,
I look into the mirror of the moon
through the window pane, filled with luminous
cold, blue and quivering
faraway reflections of worlds
cast into darkness that burn,
lonely, proud and golden,
like a series of Sanskrit marks
that resound in primordial sleep
and whisper the words of an ancient sooth
in the name of the earth, in the name of fire
from the bottom of the day lost in darkness.
This way they give back to the power of dreams
and begin rocking to give rest to hearts,
intoxicated in life's rapturous, fierce battle.
And eyes feel the touch of eyelashes
and see blue sparks.
Sleepwalkers sing on the roofs,
landscapes turn silver,
walls in rooms rustle like the forest,
and the dead moon, the blue moon
opens five gates of night
above a black and glimmering city.
The fires of streetlamps grow dark,
and silver arrows beat the window panes—
these are the arrows of stars in the heights.
Words fly from violins,
turned to stone into the beauty of despair,
and once again from a portrait, from the silver
of a picture frame painted on canvas,
my double calls to me.
Like me, he writes frenzied poems,

he recites, and sings,
and turning into a musician, the portrait,
singing, appears and vanishes.
Then the red spot of a shout
crosses lips like a spark.
Like a balsam the night pours
a sweet drop of madness
into my brain, my heart, my thoughts.

The clock strikes, two roses, a candle
and a mask—is it of death or love?
But there always is night, and the night is eternal,
the first, the thousandth, and the very last.

An open book, a lamp, wandering moths,
the rust of thoughts have lain on my heart.
On the walls shadows weave round loops
into a wondrous and tangled knot.

Like a black cat, a portly teapot sat,
a clock, like a bumble bee, hums.
How sweet is this lure of mystery and how hard
is the word seemingly made of stone!

A tin sky, a leaden moon
and the ashen smoke of the night.
Is there really no place on this earth
for unrealized and fervent fits of passion?

A bat strikes its wings on the window,
all has grown silent, calm, and cool.
The unknown lures with unrealized Eden,
like quicksilver the cold flows into your veins.

You walk, you walk, you guide strange shadows,
a song is born in your heart with pain.
The black waters of the night have begun to swim
above the world.

Go to sleep.

The hour is late.

Monday, May 1, 1933

The morning flashed. The sun like a red brick
rolled along the tin of rooftops.
The morning raked away shadows and dreams
and suddenly creaked with the song of carts.

Once again the crooked line of the falling stars
crosses out the boundless blue of the sky.
The city, wondrously white, almost incredible,
floats out of the fog as though from the imagination.

Just this nook is still embraced by shade,
a violin loosened its strings and sleeps.
Drowsy silence, just a scraping quill with wings,
buzzes like an arrow along the paper.

THE ARROW

Give me a lute made of stone,
as cold as ice and as lustrous as steel!
O, not autumn's cantilena,
the beaming, sparkling crystal of winter.

Not for nothing are ephemeral sorrows,
not milled melos, not a silky mood.
Let the strings, like flint tips,
rip my fingers and bend them till they bleed.

O, free us from the weakness of the word,
I will crush the hidden snake of treachery.
I tighten the strings and sinews,
let me nail a song like an arrow into your heart.

Thursday, April 13 and Tuesday, April 18, 1933

My days cruel and cold
have cast wormwood over my song,
horizons have drowned in the abyss
of black spring.

The tempting, intoxicating venom of words
prompts me again in my ear,
that a blizzard will swallow my heart,
albeit grudgingly.

This way in days anesthetized I will compose
this poisonous tribute to my times,
in vain: I must drink
the bitter wine of poetry on my own.

A foolish dream faithlessly calls,
I know this illusion is a phantom:
I want to carve out the face of the days
with the chisel of a poem.

People have fallen asleep in the black city,
cherishing dreams beneath their covers.
This world both boundless and cramped
will not be able to contain your dream.

Hoarse voices have grown quiet,
and peace crucifies wings,
midnight scatters poppy seeds,
this silence is not for you.

And here a small black-haired boy
raised his palms to his forehead.
No, you will not grasp the essence of the world,
you won't tear out the root of evil with a poem.

Wednesday, March 22, 1933

Midnight is black, black as coal,
a shadow moves along St. George's Square,
streaks are winding in bands
on shimmering gray walls.
The moon is a mysterious ring,
set in the ebony of night.
You'll be quivering in the silver glow
beneath the cold roof of the sky.
You can't distinguish
apparition from reality here,
is this illusion, or, perhaps,
this reality is tricky the way of a dream.
These are towers made of glass and music,
this is a fire that no longer warms,
these are the last borders of the world,
this is the architecture of reverie.
Midnight is black, black as coal,
it sprinkles the ashes of a dream on your eyes,
it sculpts the sky in long streaks,
a sky bonded to the earth.

The night resounds on St. George's Square.
The cross atop it like a mighty key.
And the undiscovered future rises
like a sullen shadow.

Friday, March 24, 1933

PART III

From the Collection
The Book of the Lion (1936)

A kingdom of dead flowers—the desert sleeps
in a golden red shirt of sand.
The stripling sedge is the devilry of foliage,
the chasing of the sun's ecstasy and lightning.

Living candles above the coffin of the earth,
stiff weeds suddenly like a burning bush.
Like bushes bent over by a hand,
the bottomless abysses of faith bend aside.

And you see eternity—an opal sky
and the fluttering of the red streams of flame.
From behind mountains of centuries the constellation
of the Lion leads, this is the sign of monarchs, of warriors, of
    prophets.

The sun darkens in a cloud of gray birds,
the laurels of a storm crown it, brown, blue,
and thunder, like the golden signature in a book,
will endure on the pages of the desert.

The signature of thunder in the royal book of lions
written by the winds from below the Sinai,
from the slopes of the mountain that embellish the brocade
spire of sands with the garland of God's lightning.

Sinai wind, strike the open playing cards!
Without you I am an empty vessel of form.
On guard all the day over a prophetic spring,
and the night is like a bible red and black.

The infused, scented black gold of nights in the desert,
lit up by violet, mixed into the salt of mosaics.
This is the red lining beneath the mantle of night. Azure gloom
    settles

                                            down
onto the oven of the earth, extinguished as you watch, though it's still
                                          hot.
Sand hills are preparing for flight like clouds of fowl
that landed to rest and that will fly off at any moment into free
                                boundlessness.
Chords upon chords,
           terraces upon terraces,
                   circles in circles,
                          distant kingdoms shine,
sardanapaluses guffaw in depravity to the tormented captive women.
A burning night of prophets. Moments cast in gold vanish.
Palms of submissive palm trees have come to the Pleiades in a sorrowful
                                    request
that the eternal rushing of the wind not torment them.
                            The monarchic roar
of the king of the desert calls to judgment before conscience from
                            beyond the gate.
The sandstorm of a musician blows into the lips of the desert. A white
                          palace of mists.
A chord to a chord,
          a blow to a blow,
                 a star against a star,
                           waves of light
from the violet of clouds, the gamut hewn into a hundred hues, the
    wings
                            of the wind.
From the cave, from among the lions, the voice of Daniel flows into
                          obscurity:

"Luminous One, Only One, who sowed a barren plant in
the majestic garden of life and warmed it with the sun of affection!
Until worms and moldiness gnaw away the meager clod of the body,
in the eternal circle of passions, in the eternal shadows of the palm
    tree
                                        of sorrow,
fighting away for meat, gold and power, always ready at any minute
to give away a crumb of luxury, the patricians of necessities,
we carry our cheap laurels and our giddy mind.
Wherever I take an unseen step, wherever there is the peril of the
    abyss,
it is You alone who will tear me out from the teeth of the Nothing,
    from
                                      the claws of fate!
When You stand by me—in the lion's den I am safe."

My ancestor swam once on the back of a whale,
for three days and three nights he preached to the depths.
A green giant—the water heavy and thick
rocked the prophet the way a mother rocks her son.

His biblical long beard—an ebony banner—
appeared to the stars from the east on bouquets of foam.
The lilies of palms stretched over the waters,
blessing dolphins swimming in the distance.

Three times the sun and moon. A good, faithful whale
swam peacefully, steadily, carefully with the prophet.
On the bed of the bottom breakers became stacked, like years,
as they pass, like the paths of the day and night.

Do you know the kingdom of darkness—the world of a million wonders,
the greenish-black homeland of the octopus?
For even a dream will not give us such images,
As a night in the sempiternal fire of the sea bottom.

Who made the monstrous shape of such beings?
A cruel joke of nature, lavish madness?
Hammerheads beat hollowly in the drift of the waters,
And sawfish carve the watery sun with a blade.

This is a second sun from the bottom—a double to the one
from beyond the clouds and its feeble shadow and hazy freakishness,
having lost its red composition—its life-giving heat,
lying in a watery grave on the rows of waves.

The first cradle of life is here, a den of elements
(when the Holy Spirit still hovered over the waters)

and the eternal grave; the sun has set there
in daily self-destruction, in daily loss!

Perhaps a terrifying ichthyosaurus still lives somewhere,
a loathsome fish-serpent, a silver-scaled dragon.
The sponges embellish medusas like cold laurels,
violets of the sea—sponges and squids—mollusks.

A drowsy sea lion rocks with dignity,
monarch of the seas, in a slippery crown of starflowers
that abundantly bloom in the watery thicket
into the oceanic springs and underwater aprils.

A floating island of flesh—a long row of fish
broke out above the beast-flowering, above the spongy meadow.
The prophet, with his hand and palm halting the flow of wind,
begins his speech in the language of the ocean:

"This is He who creates and destroys worlds,
who sent me to you, brothers from the bottom of the water, sharks!"
The sharks listen, lifting up their spines
like bows stretched to the future and the past.

"This is He, who snuffs out the night, and lights the candles of
      days,
and blesses you all with my hands!"
From the faraway Silver Waters like a cloud, sea perch
swim, striking their flippers like oars.

"This is He who tosses the wind from his palms,
He also remembers you, creatures of the horrifying deep!"
And crab after crab, like a strong, red mushroom,
grows out of the abyss and wrinkles his brow in wonder.

"This is He, who frees the sun from the ice of night,
takes care of all from the first days of the world till now!"

Here endlessly are rows upon rows of sturgeon,
behind them salmon to the borders of distant waters.

"You are blind instinct! Each of our measurements errs,
for He alone can measure without error!"
Clarity fell away, like the luster from the open stars,
that even a sheatfish ardently looks after a sheatfish.

When the mist spread out on the breasts of the sea,
The birds repeated the conversations of the sleepy waves.
Like the night, a snail of the moon's shell, crawled,
and a dolphin carried the quieted lyre of the sun to the west.

Then the prophet gave instruction to the polyps and centipedes,
who, ashamed of their horrifying, vile, black bodies,
hated the world and avenged the sin
of nature that made them so monstrous.

The dolphin swam away beyond the seventh shore of the day,
bushes of coral extinguished like evening lindens.
Then the prophet prayed and sheltered
the blessed dream of the comforted polyps.

I am already finishing this strangest of ballads
about my great grandfather and the ocean evening.
The earth in its orbit returns back
to its youth, into the phantasmagoric dream of primordial speech.

Through sabers passed I return the days
of nature to nebulousness and the first rustling of primordial days:
like a pillar of God, the night of a million years stands,
in the primordial chaos of the earth and water mixed together.

A SONG ABOUT THE LIGHT BEFORE TIME

It's no longer azure—these are already the fountains of blueness,
and the sky is fabulous—sound carved up into strips.
O flower of the body, who here is more loved than you,
as hated, as cherished and as damned as you!

A hollow wall of nothing that lies between heart and
heart, like the disturbing music of the unknown,
is this just the feeble lens of a cataract,
or is the boundlessness of the eternal too great for the heart?

Cradle of passions, o, our fetters and wings,
the sweetest chains and the most intoxicating of intoxication!
You are the power that divides us,
and the two directions of a single rudder of human decisions.

The raw bell of the azure swoons from the swelter
and blood of the wind—light pours out of the cracks.
That the eternal dream of delusions weaves from the macula of
    mosaics,
I drink and, drinking, strive with my entire heart all the more.

Terraces of light—the scales of the loftier sounds each time
one over another rise up above the moss like gloom.
—A downpour of azure falls on weakened hands.
This is the sky falling, a heavenly catastrophe!

I pray to the earth in the red boiling of blood
and I call the sky with a sadness that eternally wounds.
From my pagan lips Christ's song flows,
like wine from the water of Cana in Galilee.

She, leaning against the stone wall of the well, ponders—a chipped lyre
made of stone stumps, where the Unearthly Foreigner had gone.
Like strings, streams tuned to the scale of changing sounds
worriedly repeating a thought about the wants of this world.
Who is he—that hireling of working servants of the Lord's vineyard?
She bends over the curb of the well and her azure blue and white soul
seems completely pure and calm, like the calmest of flowers bending
over a flower.
A reed-pipe with a reed-pipe, a sister with a sister, they shyly
convey something, and worriedly, tollingly, and instructively.
The sun moves along alleys of chords into the distant garden of a
musician.

A herd of sheep floats in the white milk of their wool,
the month of flowers passes—the blossom of his roses!—filled with
light.
The azure and white. The banter of reed-pipes. The blowing of the wind.
The time of defeat shifts to blooming, the time of the bitter seed
approaches.
The wind from the shore tells good news to the grass
and gray bunches of ashes already are ripening in rough stumps.
In defense of the Muses—a blessed meadow—the sun is rising among
the birds
and obliging insects ardently celebrate the right of honey.

All the same beauty, though simple and cunning, will not quench the
heart
with water for which we no longer strive. It's entirely different!
The water of beauty teaches us to strive higher, more subtly, and brighter.
This stream just flows through us, we do not create it,
we are just a vessel, at that, a humble vessel that receives beauty.
And once again thirsting we strive for beauty that we create

in our soul ourselves in the fruitful effort of freely chosen burning
and the grace of living water that alone is all-calming.

When here with your heart you rush for the Inspiration-lipped
    Foreigner,
bend down, faraway sister, over the precious stream of the Word
and give some living water to me—the heir of your thirst!

The night slipped down like the cape from Christ's shoulders,
from the pierced side of the heavens light pours out.
The wounds of thorny stars on the mountain still fester, and from
    beneath
the gloom will wash away the fully bloomed bare feet of the day.

The earth, as though newly born of nothing,
rolls out from behind the dark mountains of chaos.
I baptize each small flower with a new name
and kill each one with it unwittingly.

And each flower becomes reborn tenfold
and shines again unnamed beneath the dew,
and the sun—a musician's diamond, a feast day of light—
will double the world for eyes that want to comprehend all.

By two, by three, by a hundredfold,
until I comprehend: it is not for me to capture things
in the cage of the word. I lie down on a green bed,
hungry for an apple from the earth and sated with light.

The dew flows in hyssop—a golden foam,
and a noble current flows into the vessel of the body.
The motionless bottom, the imperishable firmament, gazes through
the flow of things into silver ecstasies and carries sound across.

For only sudden rapture can uncover essence,
can join us into a mystical union with the world.
A heaven nailed to the cross of the earth sighs
and the stigmata of the sun shine on my palm.

ROSES

The time of roses is late, sister,
we've waited so long and now it's coming.
The earth and water have been measured
into the miles of sun and versts[1] of light.

Though this light is overly weak,
though it's too early and the snow persistent,
the sparing sun and the verdure bare,
all the same the day is abundant in spells.

Washing your hand in the blood from the roses,
to the first cooing of turtledoves,
we walk, amid the beech trees, a faraway
star with star and heart with heart.

1 A now obsolete form of measurement equivalent to a little more than a kilometer.

Green shadows. Carnations—
ambassadors of spring. Get totally smashed!
How great this world has become again!
And once again I read your letters.

Overhead a green hole of light,
a kernel—an electric carnation.
No, we aren't accustomed to the fact yet
that our youth is not forever.

But we'll get used to it at some point . . .
For the time being there is sacred deception—
that friendship with life will not vanish,
that anoints us, my love, with the chrism of spring.

The red youth of peonies.
What beauty! What intoxication!
Take my brow into your palm
and protect it, my vernalelation!

For it chases me through the gloom—
another step, another,
it will hit me on the mark,
my best friend and my most avid enemy, dear Lord!

Dark inspiration, eternal muse!
The night strikes the black bells of shadows.
On a black background, like tragic blood,
the red youth of peonies.

The red gold of tulips
on a gray sun—a tray made of bast
and the mechanical garden of melodies
where a musician slumbers in black disks.

The prisoner of metal—the human voice
is condemned to an empty circle,
and the prisoner of the world—the human heart
incapable of fathoming it.

Through gray silk—gray dullness
the red gold of tulips.
To bloom, to burn and to pass,
to forsake everything, going into the unknown!

Violets and a telephone receiver
call with an enchanting glow,
and the moon, like a red sponge,
washes away the ashes of the day from your face.

A snail made of ebony, a dark seashell
and the ear of the night—a black funnel,
redolent fragrances stifle,
like fingers on the throat of a clarinet.

From the eyes of the violets you crumble with sorrow
and embrace, morning sister!

Outstretched palms of silence
above our eternal fading.

The red cubes of walls, the circles of yellow town squares, the squares
of parklets.
Man, lay out the stars and cities with the compass of thought!
Block upon block, a circle in the circle, windows above windows and
doors,
The sun rises on brass stairs like a golden statue.

Pools like unmoving mirrors in red dust.
Here the sky bathes in water thick and silver like mercury.
In the green flame of grass marble steeds graze,
Stone angels metallically blow their trumpets in the park.

Heroes descend from their pedestals, sparks scatter from trombones,
and the sun on a cannon, and the flags of museums on fire,
and lions from the flags majestically walk through the city in rows,
and the marble leader on a curly-haired steed.

A marble tenor has already been singing on the theater
square to the golden stars for two hundred years.
When at the command of the night spindles stand still,
gray smoke swathes textile workshops grown quiet.

Young girls return home from the looms
and in lustful fantasies dream of passionate tenors,
how they wildly pamper them and wash their throats with song,
and red-headed tomcats treacherously fawn over them.

The master of the city is the lion who sleeps beneath the arsenal,
rising up slowly, he walks into the desert of city squares.
The heroes sleep, they are still singing in houses of ill repute,
and the rain rings freedom for rebels in the prisons.

On the square of brass angels wrapped in silence,
when the darkness pours out red ink,
a historian writes about the past from a pedestal
and dips his quill pen into an inkwell.

Silhouettes of heavy stonefooted prisons
Grown into the earth rise up as giant sleepy lions,
and lovers and comets visit the prisoners at night,
and the moon crawls slowly along the wall like a spider.

When words are rubbed into dust it's useless to confess to the stars.
On the stars, as though on walls, there are mildew, worms, mold, and
dampness.
The moon washes the faces of the prisoners with a cold and blue glow,
until they are covered overnight like round stumps with a rough moss.

The slippery spectral herbs of underground rivers, wet stars and snakes,
the valleys of the moon overgrown with a chestnut grove.
For a hundred days and a hundred nights red rains fall and wind blows,
the water rises and floods the stars and prisons.

Where stone did not remain on stone, where mountains were leveled,
masons again are building a new prison from flowery blocks.
The crimson flower of the mandrake blossoms beneath the gallows,
and the rope of the hanged men brings happiness to the living.

Waters filled with living silver, the wells of compassion are sleeping,
the wells of eternal compassion that touched these walls.
Already the flight of the gait no longer takes them into the laurel of
                                                                    defeat,
neither does the bustling racket awaken a forum of trifles.

In the cistern of the night future stars of the morning wash
    themselves,
busts of the sun from a mane in flames in the museum of the night.
Already the hoarfrost of years silverplates the ruins. As though a link
                                                            along a chain,
the slow wind pushes clouds and time splashes mildew.

Plaited tightly shoulder to shoulder, hawthorn bushes go on,
green springs from the bowels of the earth, where the momentary life
of marketplaces gurgles, where minutes swarmed.
The shadow of a cloud fell onto the cemetery of golden monarchies.

The queen of ecstasy—the night leads words through a stone meadow
between the laurels, where music floats mysteriously from the petals,
and a nightingale, the brother of a star, sings of the death of his sister.
A tragic wind calls on the empty stage of the world.

Where a marble steed with milk grown cold from its mane
with a powerful neighing awakens distant Troys in vain.
Soulless goldfinches peck out a grain from the eyes of the heroes.
Starlion sets beyond the shadow of a golden time.

The deepest blue of all the blue wonders—the sky beyond,
that, like a fire from beyond the gloom, shines from behind the
    night.
Someone led the stars to the sky somewhere,
guess whether it is a dream, or your heart, or if it is whispering!

The deepest blue of all blue nights—is ours.
Someone somewhere, call out with me!
This song will not betray us—silver smoke and a chalice,
I give my oath of loyalty before the face of the stars.

He who enters the world without a star—remains without one
    forever.
He who has not made peace with life—is always alone!
A star shears its silver braids on the grave of truth,
and, like dark bunches of grapes, sorrowful days hang above.

Bitter art is like foam on the libation of beauty,
and the Muse who cares for her lion cub in the garden,
who leads her chosen ones to intoxicating merchantry,
to sell to the nights all that is in their souls.

You ask how these poems—myths were born,
how the mythmaking Muse acts through her influence:
the ruins of crimson kingdoms rise in dust to the light,
an unearthly kingopolis—a Magic-opolis above the gulf.

Twelve rivers flow through this nightingale city,
a keeper of the winds blows into a thin shepherd's flute,
a white wall of music and winged news of arrows,
a stately lion, a weak human being, and faithful stars.

The bronze lake of a desert and scraggy cliffs,
the red and remote plains of lethargy.
Lilies of rising stars bow down to the desert,
that lifts up manes of sandstorms in a threatening way.

The empty and hole-filled shell of the sun
that kills itself like a scorpion
with the stinger of its rays and on red thickets
its winged soul freed from its form
soars in the expanses all the way beyond a green land,
behind the wall of a hundred nights that are phosphorous and black
and will rest in sleepy and extinct volcanoes.

Here is the cradle of storms fallen asleep in rock cribs,
here winds are born that in time on a hundred wings
will bend the banners of a red glow above the east.
A nest of eagles of the defeat of those driven
from primordial paradise adorn a bald spire,
where lilies of rising stars and playful pearls of wasps
meet the bronze night in the thin, barely noticeable glass of the sky.
The sands like a red cape in the bosom of the desert
have torn off into flight, have fallen and grown still.

And only the thoughtful and wise ichneumons,[1]
who place their ears to the lyres of the wind, hear the mysterious
and distant call of underground bells.
The sands and stars swirl in whirlpools
and the cliffs slap like masts in the wind.
The desert like a lioness half asleep and half awake,
dried up, she breathes in the reddish ash,

---

1 Killers of dragons and crocodiles; also known as the "mongoose" and "otter."

like clouds of sulfur and chalk.
Jackals wallow on waves of sand,
their eyes, like coins of madness, have fallen
into the outflow of a dust cloud and into the pit of madness.
These are ancient cities awakening beneath the sands.

Tattooed girls dance on the city square of reverie,
sand burning underfoot, like red tar, melts, and from more than
a hundred hundred years I carve the dance of the sun on a tambourine,[1]
two staffs clap like the wings of a bird that swoons from intoxication.
Flashing with my farewell song, I expire like a sleepy cloud,
a fern will cover the dances of the girls, like the earth's palm.
Strange round dances return from the highlands of silence and bow
their faces made of bronze beneath bouquets of an evening fire.

Beyond the shores of sorrow, where the eternal green night has lain
                                                    down,
beyond seven mountain summits
                        and seven seas,
                                    red buffaloes
majestically descend to a mysterious land to the underground
meadows, where the departed sun will shine for them—an ebony disk.

1 This line can also be read as "I carve a dance on the tambourine of the sun."

Having wandered into thickets, wrapped in the wind,
covered by the sky and swaddled in songs,
I lie like a wise fox beneath the blossom of a fern,
and I ripen, grow cool, and harden into white stone.

A green flood of plant life rivers rises,
the endless clatter of hours, comets and leaves.
The flood envelops me, crushes me with the white sun,
and my body will become charcoal, my song will turn to ashes.

Thousands of centuries will roll past like lava,
where we once lived, palm trees that have no name will grow,
the charcoal from our bodies will bloom as a black flower,
and pick-axes in a quarry will ring into my heart.

Not for meager silver, not for liquor,
not for dubious and double-meaning laurels,
not for the salt of playful sallies,
not for success in the game for heedless risk,
not for the honey of golden-tongued lips,
not for the sweet manna of honors
and not even for a bouquet of virtues,
whose radiance time and again is deceptive,
not for the dark juice of grapes
in a friendly circle over tea,
not for anointment by the muses, that for a lifetime
designates a person with a mark,
not conceived in a cunning way,
to measure souls, a learned cubit,
not for the lazy smoke of households,
or for the slick music of two-faced boasting,
not for the shelter of dreams—for blessed home,
but instead we pray to the distant stars
so that in this world we would be given
a grand and suffering life.

Superstitions of past ages—of
sparkling dreams burn like a bonfire.
The city of my youth is
in the red taffeta of sunset.

Stars chatter atop poplars
and people cross themselves when troubled,
when Hassidim in black synagogues
stab at the moon with knives . . .

My mysterious town is
in the curtain of boyhood recollections!
And again bygone youth calls
the way old superstitions call.

THE TALE[1] OF A BLACK REGIMENT

A tale clangs against a tale—prophetic bits of bronze.
—I sing, I do not curse
the routed regiments, the jagged ranks, the smashed cohorts!
Praise to all who with passion kiss their sister on battlefields,
and to those, who fear, like a snail in its shell, who crouch the canes of
their backs, scorn!

The echo of defeat beats about my ears, like the betrayals of thunder
from the depths of the abyss, broken into bits and seized into a net, a
farewell grievance.
I gaze into the gloom, how the bowstrings of cliffs, having strained the
bows of waterfalls,
like arrows stretched tautly, all of a sudden toss out crooked-beaked
birds.

The day is breaking. The regiment in retreat. Anabasis beneath the
African sky.
The forest of lances stuck at the sky pricks the moon, reddish blood
flows from it,
and the ebony leader with a star earring in his ear, pagan singing
flinging into the clouds like a challenge, curses the defeats of a wicked
god.

There is no mercy—and bayonets stick into a body, like plows into the
chornozem,[2]
into the tempestuous field of black bodies bayonets sow the seed of
obedience and harmony,
so that to the seventh generation they would remember and that each
would know forever,

1 I have translated *Slovo* here (literally meaning "word") as "tale," as in the famous epic
poem "The Tale of the Host of Ihor" (Igor in Russian).
2 The famous rich black earth of Ukraine.

so that a son would, like a treasure, retell to his grandson, a grandson to his descendant how they fortified their power.

They are thickly spread up against each other like a pristine forest
                                                                chopped down,
their brains gurgle in their crushed skulls like yellow oil.
He who sows blood will reap hate. Take this baptism of steel!
Green-eyed black princes, Muse of avengers, stir the puddles!

Dragons that drink gasoline are like birds and rhinos,
dragons that spit out venom—oil and grainy fire,
they appear as if they had returned from the caves of the moon, and
beneath their feet the broom of a comet raising up dust, sweeping
                                                                away people like leaves.

On piles of black arms and black legs there is red blood and yellow
    foam,
a slippery deadly foam from lips tortured by a cannon's kiss.
Tulips of the underground depths—the mines, like fiery bushes, burst,
invincibly and resonantly greeting with their salutes from the depths of
                                                                the earth.

Cannons spread fans of smoke like wings before flight,
heaps of bodies and steel debris break loose and trample with their
                                                                wheels, on black jaws
the sticky saliva of death, eyes glued with sweat, the tongue of a reddish
star licks dust from the iron-plate and vileness from mouths and the
                                                                dirt of blood.

Throats hollowly wheeze, loathsome asthma crookedly contorts fingers,
plaited palms are like leaves—flowers trampled by the thirst of life
ignite for the last time and theomachists fling curses at the sky.
All treasures for a single moment of life! Just the night heals everyone
                                                                forever.

The shovel of the sun sinks into the warm yellow gravelly soil, digging
                                                                    the graves,
the shovel of the sun, a cross of graceful winds, the burial rite of jackals.
O black body, in the reddish silk of sand swathed, tranquil and feeble,
where just before the moment passions still seethed! Good palm of the
                                                                    earth!

Let the black Mother of God from the fire-icon lead the warriors to
    their
                                                                    land,
where dragons will no longer frighten, where there is eternal silence and
                                                                    dreamy waters!
A tale beats against a tale—bits of bronze resound.
Thus we finish our farewell song,
while the shattered black regiment
                            departs
                                    to the land of stars
                                            to eternal night.

February 1936

PART IV

From the Collection
The Green Gospel (1938)

PART IV

From the Collection
The Green Gospel (1978)

FIRST CHAPTER

Of all phenomena, the most wondrous is existence.

The day already is burning on the coal of night,
evening washes ashes from the grass with dew,
and fear grinds your heart like a drill,
and the moon will frighten away lost shadows.

My lonely friend, as in a sash of night,
you are wrapped in the mysteriousness of the world.
Go with me this spring evening
to drink liquor in the tavern on the moon.

1931

The laws of "bios" are the same for everyone:
birth, suffering and death.
What will be left after me: ashes of my words,
what will be left after us: grass will grow from bones.

Foxes, lions, swallows, and people,
the worms and leaves of a green star,
all is subject to the immutable laws of matter,
just as the sky above us is blue and silver!

I understand you, fauna and flora,
I hear comets howl and grass growing.
Antonych is an animal, too, a sad and curly-haired one.

May 18, 1935

The greenish grains of flax rustle in chests,
a greasy and warm dust swirls in oil presses.
Each time in the heavy rooted lindens a green soul,
wrathful and troubled, will flash through a curse.

The frantic flow of life does not acquiesce to the worms,
woodpeckers strike green sparks from the trees.
The evening stingily pays the day for the sun with the
gold coin of a star, that it will comb out into red moss.

The red soot of sunset covers the lindens,
that round, like sieves, sow sleepy seeds,
and strings of leaves grow silent with a sudden sob
beneath the touch of wind that trampled the silence with a rustle.

The girls from the oil presses faintly smell of flax,
when, like a flower, they open up their bodies to their lovers,
and the sun bursts in a mad chiming,
drunkenly striking into the sonorous plates of clouds.

It suddenly grows quiet in the mad hymn,
like pumice that floats to the surface in oil,
and frenzied and irrepressible streams pour out into the roots

of bodies, into the veins of lindens, into the thickets of groves.
Look, this is the wildfire of the world, a storm of the elements,
plants pray, each color rages,
underground winds blow from below into the roots,
until a linden, like a clarinet, first begins to play solo.

Here are the chimneys of the earth, here trees emit smoke
in a green, golden and crimson color.

In the straw of the mist stumps, summits in a farewell
blizzard of the sun that has set behind them like a bird.

And to the sunset and summer and dreamy lindens,
to the eternal volatility of the world in evening and morning,
I give glory to the ceaseless labor in the oil-press,
to the blazing of souls, to the ecstasy of bodies and to the high of
    lovers.

December 11, 1935

FIRST LYRIC INTERMEZZO

When the stone still sang, serpents had wings,
and Eve wore bird cherry leaves,
then a brisker and more intoxicating wind blew,
and the sea shone in silver beneath the stars.

When Eve tore off the moon from the apple tree,
the stormy-maned lions in paradise rebelled.
The sons of Adam scattered throughout the world,
raising cities and palaces for Eve.

April 4, 1935

We will go ahead of us, embracing,
into the evening, into the horizon, into song.
The wind tears stars from the heaven
like tiles from roofs.

And, distancing ourselves from the throng,
we will wrap ourselves in the fur of night.
Let two hearts—two doves
in harmony and in mourning begin to flutter.

April 3, 1935

He was in love with art and an artist in love,
he hewed arrow-spired churches and charmed women,
he hewed inspired words and played on a florid fiddle.
Young girls and women blazed in drunken happiness.
O, more than one girl has lost her garland!

When he died his works remained:
sonorous songs and silver-domed churches.
Deacons sang as well as choirs,
the churches were adorned in silver pines.
There twenty of his best lovers
lamented in the curly-haired morning.

April 4, 1935

THE FAIR

My brother—a tailor of boyhood dreams—
sewed together the sky to the earth.
The tradesmen's scarves blaze
like a comb of a hundred colors.

The carpenters are singing, tambourines are beating.
I will reveal a mystery:
the red sun is being sold
at the fair in Horlytsia.

January 20, 1935

SECOND CHAPTER

Beyond the dam of three days and three nights, where there is a
    numbing
                                                        whirlpool,
there is a bottomless abyss of green in the halfsleepy halfbeing of
                                                        infinitude.
Tied to the tree stumps, chained winds and the god of fear,
a hundred-faced, clever god, who always has a new face.

Close to the earth lightning streak-snakes skate along the stumps,
slippery from the dew, that, like milk, congeals into enamel.
The squandering night destroys an excess of forms like unwanted stains,
just the oak, like a miser, keeps the leaves of green coins.

Leaning on a ray of light as though on a cane, a star stands above the
                                                        ravine,
where like a badger in its den, evil has hidden and has grown quiet.
The boundary lines of the mire smelled of fumes, mold smolders in a
                                                        red fire,
and the night like a black buffalo, the moon in horns—a wisp of fur.

A mad number of forms. Wealth intended for specters,
and up high the desert of the sky—human fear and rapture, dead light,
just the oak—a plant life lion above the forest, a proud and miserly
                                                        monarch,
leads the scepter of the sun in the morning above a prodigal world.

June 9, 1936

Slowly we return to the ground as though to the cradle.
Green knots of herbs bind us—two hobbled chords.
The ax of the sun is stuck in an oak stump, with the blade of
    radiance,
the music of moss, the caress of the wind, the oak is proud, like an
    idol.

On the raft of the day that carries us, obedient and warm bodies
merge together like two dreams, two faithful flowers.
Like cat's fur, moss warms us. You trade the stars for a whisper,
you trade blood for the verdure and music. The sky is glowing.

Where you find the day's shore, beyond the sea of sky, future winds
    sleep
and our faithful stars—our fates await beyond the seas,
until on the commands of the earth they are realized. We cast away
everything inessential and take only pure ecstasy to the stars.

The inspiration of the blood hurts. Eyebrows prick like two arrows,
and a wall of melody above is like a great moon,
like a wing of the winds. Our destiny depends on the stars.
You burn plantlike and thirsty, like the earth. You are entirely music.

May 18, 1936

THE GARDEN
(A BIOLOGICAL POEM IN TWO VARIANTS)

I.

Words tremble, like bees in the rain,
a conversation, barely begun, breaks off,
thoughts flash and hide quickly
and a glance, like a butterfly, is winged and clear.

The room for us will turn into a flowering garden
and we will intertwine, embracing each other like curly-haired leaves.
I will grow, like a root into you and the dew will flash
in our lucid dreams, flickered in silver.

II.

Two of us—two shaggy and intertwined bushes
and our smile—is a tender butterfly with wings.
Pinned thoughts, like bees in the rain,
tremble. strongly pierced on sharp thorns.

Songs, like berries, every day flicker
that garden where we grow, tightly embracing the leaves.
The vegetative god of love, primordial and pure,
fills everything here in the depth, all the way to the roots.

March 15, 1935

SECOND LYRIC INTERMEZZO

Already the night warmed by intoxicated flowers
smokes in a bird cherry haze,
and letters shine like stars
in an open book on the desk.

This desk gets overgrown with wild leaves
and along with the chair I am already a bush.
From the bird cherries I read—from hundred-leafed books—
the plant life wisdom of eternal wilderness.

March 21, 1935

A SERMON TO THE FISH

To the crucians, to the carp and to the dolphins,
to all my brothers from the sweet and salt waters:
"Do not give us either roe or whalebone,
we strive for your open spaces, freedom and adventure."

The water is heavy, and the sky even heavier than the water.
That is why your depth allures us,
enchants and calls us temptingly,
your coral god from the bottom of the sea.

April 4, 1935

Carp sing and their blades cut the waters,
wind lifts roofs, like lids of trunks,
and a birch tree gives a sermon to a perch.
This is all unreal, even unbelievable,
don't believe it!

And real is what I saw in the morning
where the river washes the roots of a grove,
when the winds, like passionate lovers,
undress girls for bathing.

April 4, 1935

Antonych grows, and the grass grows,
and curly alder trees are greening,
O, bend over, just bend over,
you'll hear the most mysterious of all words.

Spring, don't distress us with April rain!
Who has crushed the azure sky like a glass jug,
who is scattering the leaves—bits of glass at you?
Do you want to catch rain into a sieve?

Of all, the language of meadows is the most wondrous;
someone loaded star-bullets into the rifle of the night,
cuckoo birds on the alders will peck away the moon,
Antonych grows, and the grass grows.

Antonych was a May-bug and once lived on cherry trees,
on those cherry trees of which Shevchenko[1] sang the praises.
My starry land, biblical and abundant,
the flowery homeland of the cherry tree and nightingale!

Where evenings are out of the Gospels, where there are dawns,
where the sky overwhelmed white villages with the sun,
the inspired cherry blossoms are blossoming curly and with a high,
just as in Shevchenko's day they are steeping the song with hops
    again.

April 16, 1935

---

1 The great bard and national poet of Ukraine Taras Shevchenko (1814–1861).

THIRD CHAPTER

A rain of raspberries falling. Tribes of bees raving. Strings of light
plucked. The envoys have arrived from Goldsea.
A quartet of palms—two hobbled chords. Brooms of mist.
A white steed enters into a red rain of berries. The envoys speak

of the stars, their language beyond understanding.
Long ago my mother used to sing of Goldsea,
an underwater kingdom where the sun sleeps in white villas
in a downpour of light. The cart is moving—seven-starred wheels.

This is the day departing. The string of the palm plays. It quiets in a
                                                                handshake.
The red youth of the raspberry slowly turns ashen.
Slowly you enter into a dream as if going back to the cradle,
Feather beds of moss on the forest bed. Shadows of fans.

In a star's lips the reed of a flute. The night adorns foreheads,
obedient to the laws of passion. The oak is sacred. A doe dashes.
You lie on the fur of night warm and devoted. The wise circle
of life is crowned. Only love is stronger than death.

May 24, 1936

Let the two of us journey for the enchanted fleece.
From the hand of the wind that waved farewell to us, a clod
of an extinguished star fell as a gift.
Onward! Seven miles of love and the last—of sorrow.

Poetry and a storm in the whirlwind of images.
The ribbon of the road is tied into a knot of the sun.
I bow down to you, o lady of the curling dust,
that you ring with the disk of years, shapely epic muse!

Two horses made of snow and foam and the dark bottom of love,
you have taken my life into your fingers like a little ball,
and we will rest only at the fifth mile
on the burdock leaf of the young sun.

Lilies made of milk and song above the precipice
where sleepy bogs nest and gurgle.
Here is the eighth mile of sorrow and lips that burn
more heatedly than a star and briefer than a moment.

January 8, 1936

We—are the tempters of girls, of persuasive lovers,
we, who bartered our darlings like bright-colored shellfish,
for those who gave us to drink of love's thornapple,
unfortunate souls, we will pray for our victims!

At the bottom a slippery and wet moon—a wedding ring,
and the sun here is as cold as an extinguished stone.
Underwater dancers, our ancient sisters,
embrace the dolphins with their dead arms.

O you, who lay out the sea with the stars and moss,
do not take the girls from their blossoming shellfish into the sky,
convey upon them the greatest grace—the forgetting of everything,
change the white souls of drowned girls into coral!

March 17, 1935

The boat of the sun moored at the pier—at a window on the oak
and tossed seven red oars in farewell.
Pillars of slender poplars have held up the sky. Lips grow silent.
Ambassadors had come from the night. Will you go, young
   carpenter?

Where your brother—an idol in the vineyards on clouds
cares for juicy bunches of stars in a garden made of floating linen
   cloths,
when the guelder rose in the evening becomes slightly dulled,
like the doors of music, cliffs of light opened up.

You lift up your eyes—azure berries in the abyss,
like the first cuneiform scribe, you copy the laws of harmony.
Silver tallow is ablaze in the night-lamps of cold stars,
and snakes, like green candles, shine with the wax of poison.

Your steed, like a black flame, like captured wind,
just the milk of its mane flows down along its pliant neck,
it paddles with its leg, like an oar and to the call of distant paths
it widens its nostrils. We have hearts that eternally tear apart in two
and yellow human flowers—brains in skulls, as though they were in
   jars.

May 18, 1936

Broad-shouldered stumps. Worms and June.
Oak leaves strew silver dust from
extinguished stars. The bottom
of underground rivers. The first of plants tremble.

A kerchief of tiny clouds on the face of the sky.
Worms sleepily sing a hymn of decay.
A morning arch, like a sunny eyebrow.
Large lumps of rays—thin-stemmed rays.

A green turret—an arrow-tipped oak,
having risen up out of the black plank-beds of night,
it hunts worms and the fire of decay
a stubborn god pours out in fresh sap.

The electricity of the green earth
fills the plants like living bronze,
but you—proud plant, as well,
that sings this, not knowing why,
when, like a stump, overcome by decay,
will roll to the blue clods of the earth.

May 1, 1936

A wagon drives into the third dam of the night. Who, wind, is it calling
us?
Will the white sunrise soon come out to meet us like a deer from the
pinewood?
And for me you are wondrous, and I am mysterious for myself.
My cart, like a bird, raises two wings of dust with the wind beside it.

Give the cards, queen of April, give the cards and read from my palm!
I drive into the joy of the day, I drive into the sadness of the night, do
you hear me, heart?
Eh, you do not hear, no! Then let's play cards! Your heart will ache in
the bosom
of bottomless spring! Strew the wind into dreams and strew the stars,
like bits of glass!

Then let's play the dark cards of fate! Even if they're, perhaps, the cards
of death.
Come to me, slender princess, in your diamond way judge between me
and the wind!
Two of us are too many today. And both of us are stubborn.
Give me a minute, give me a minute! It's useless to warm your fingers
beneath the stars.

My home is beyond the third star. My love is waiting for me there.
The wrapped night descends in the tatters of a dream thinner than
beams,
nailed to the earth with the stars, where the last nightingales
splash till morning, and who wash their wings in the rising sun.

In the pink fingers of the morning star a card of sorrow will begin to
quiver and wither!
Give a moment to get high! Revel in the beauty of you to the loss of
consciousness,

and toss the card of sorrow—the card of evil, into a well, lady in pink,
lead my wagon through the mountain above all the treacherous pits!

The valley of the third cock's crows. The morning flapping of
                                        goldfinches in the azure,
Dew on gray flowers—a film made of golden glue.
From the petals of palms words fly wrapped in youth;
my love, the wind, the lady of diamonds, and the home beyond the star.

February 13, 1936

The hymn of plant life streams that calls for the irrepressibility of
    growth,
and the heart, as though after a seventh drink, is incredibly high.
I'll be leaving now. I've been just an occasional guest here.
I'll be praying to other stars and waiting for other mornings.

Ready to burst, buds swell in a sticky foam,
as stars meeting plants in a kiss stick,
and through funnels of violets the night filters spring magic,
and sprinkles handfuls of fragrances into the cups of flowers.

The green night of plants is stifling with the rapture of languor,
in spasms of splendor, bushes, roots, fingers, and leaves,
the seeds explode, and the moon pierces the earth with its horn,
until it expires, covered by the day that glistens like a kite beyond it.

The roots knotted and juicy in the skulls of dead men,
life drives in knotty drills into the nests of death,
and an oak bounds over to an oak—two angry gods,
striking with driving force into the stump, they obstinately intertwine.

Shining circles whirl—uncatchable reels,
here is the good news of the dawn—and the sun will grind the night.
Quaff the seventh drink of joy! Let your heart be high and winged!
Let your poetry be wise and seething, like the verdure!

I live a brief moment. Whether I'll live longer, I don't know,
so I learn getting high from the plants, the growth and the rushing flow
                                       of sap.
Perhaps my home is not here.
                        Perhaps it is beyond a star.
                                      As long as
I am here, I feel this instinctively: I sing—therefore I am.

Beneath the shell of the earth rushing waters gurgle,
the horizon in violet mists beyond the morning as though beyond a
    wall.
I will leave now with my palms on the lyre of the rising sun,
singing the praise of superhuman and plant life storms.

March 7, 1936

PART V

From the Collection
Rotations (1938)

The alleys of sounds rush, planted into scales.
As though upon a chord, a floor fell upon a floor.
The dams of yellow walls, the daily clamor of streets
from shore to shore, the shadow of oak crowns.

The day sparkles like a glass of golden tea,
the azure cleaned through, the froth of gloom above.
The people of the yellow cities walk and their eyes gleam,
though they deeply hide their sorrow like bitter seeds.

Churches, candy stores, hitching posts for the spirit and body.
For the stars and coins. Waiting for rare crumbs
of fragile happiness, we will sense other goals.
Like a probe into a wound, despair weighs heavily on our souls.

But behind the wall is jazz and the dances of lampions,
a ballet of tiny balls, the choir of colors like a choir of oboes,
and the yellow breasts of immense stadiums
sigh mutely, trampled by the blustery throng.

And smoke spreads to your feet—the birds resigned,
and the sun like a spider, having crucified the red web of antennae
on the slanting arch of walls,
catches and kills sounds like dead flies.

The artists of the plants are tulips, looking after form,
falling to their knees, colorfully and beautifully they will wither,
and by the laws of formulae unknown to us,
the days and cities bustle, and drills bustle.

Wires quiver like nerves. A warm white tiny leaf,
a star in an envelope, several words and the bloom of the wild rose.

They circle like crumpled leaves, the dreams of dentists
above the vortices of a drill's monotonous melodies.

June 11, 1936

Oak leaves, the scales of vendors, gypsies,
the daily racket and every night eternal stars.
Life that is the most difficult of the arts. A reprimand
for every superfluous day. The night is waiting—a harsh judge.

Sweet-worded lips will betray. Perhaps a recollection
will not be left from the worries that have plowed our brows.
The wing of a cape from shoulders. The wing of winds above a house,
knots of smoke that bind the sky with the circle of the city.

Heroes, perverts, poets, really,
the virtue of the blossom and stains on the bed sheet,
days and nights, the delectation of shamefaced boys
and the jokes of card dealers, the dark holes of sadness.

Somewhere a barrel organ screeches endlessly, long bands of light
swirl on faces like peacock feathers,
and in the crooked beak of a parrot human fate
sways like a piece of cheap paper:
love,
      a trip,
            parting,
                  fame,
                        success—
for twenty cents you can buy happiness.
The smile of the day plaits and unplaits,
the parrot, the song and the golden communion of the sun.

Unexpected meetings. Orchestras play in the parks.

Virtuous families with many children pass.
An evil wind that wracked human despair with inspiration
is already growing silent. Bunches of cards and the flight of clouds.

The shadow of the wings of fate. A fragile cane and the sacrifices of
flowers.

And we capture the flow of inspiration in numbers,
we dress
the odd strangeness of the smallest of matters into compact and obstinate
truths,
though just the wisdom of ecstasy alone is infallible.

May 20, 1936

Where, wringing blue hands,
the night calls for help in vain,
drunks and shadows stagger
next to a hobbled street lamp.

Stooping like an azure flower,
the street lamp withers like a lily,
and the world is unreal, it is just mice
leading drunken shoemakers to the moon.

In the tavern with stars and bells,
where the con men and chimney-sweeps
sing hymns over their glasses
and glorify the night and the allure of temptation.

A tormenting bitch the lady of sorrow,
bending down to the bankbreakers,
with a face wrinkled like a sponge,
contorting counterfeit cards in her fingers.

Leaning their elbows in thought,
favorites of the nocturnal trade
float on the linen cloth of smoke and noise
to the chatter of stars in a violin case.

In a nest of illusions, raving, outrage
to the sobbing of candles—parrots tell fortunes
for con men to tremulous birds
and words sink into the table like nails.

The cutthroats cry out of folly
and confess to the liquor,

and, like a spider, a forgotten song
torn into bits crawls into the throat.

Once again the chimney-sweeps with the banner
of a hymn will begin to mutter the praise of life.
Who is this who suddenly slammed into the tankard
. . . . ?

Drinking glasses, like birds, fly up
over the tables, beneath the ceiling,
clapping with their glass wings,
they play with bells above the deep blue
bush of smoke that covers the tavern.

The last star has already faded
and the moon also had to fade,
and in the broken shell of a skull
the choir of con men and chimney-sweeps
murmur and chatter till morning.

January 30, 1936

Men in gray overcoats drown in the deep blue of an alley,
and the shadow smudges a young girl, like images effaced.
Golden tea in a glass. You so want to lean
against the edge of the window and drink the strong, tart and blue cold,
to look as a sad star parts with a final kiss
with her sister, who, in her stargazecircle
will no longer
    shine.
        This way the night
with azure snow washes the poppies of melancholy in the city.
Covering stooped shoulders with the sheepskin coat of the sky,
a chauffeur rocks back and forth in a sleepy limousine.
A crooked lamppost—a broken flower and the ashes of snow,
and light—green tallow poured from the jug of the night into twilight,
crooked and dark steps, a coat filled with holes, a lost droplet of
  laughter
and the moon—a white bird of evil inspiration,
and the silk bullet of daydreaming cutthroats hidden in shadows,
that, perhaps, someday will touch your heart the way one touches a
  string.
It will touch and kiss proudly and tenderly, and forever
will close your open eyes, like your last sister.
Men in gray overcoats pull out stars from their pockets
and pay their young ladies for five minutes of love.
Putting on their stooped shoulders the deep blue fur of the sky,
a chauffeur rocks in a sleepy limousine.

December 13, 1935

Spectral stone buildings and boxes of courtyards,
like thickets of gloom, wet and narrow steps,
the abyss of the night that no one has measured,
and the sadness of dark gates, and the languorous scent of mold.

A crumpled and bespattered bit of paper,
a brief and simple note: "No one is to blame,
don't look for the guilty party!" The moon is walking in quiet bast
    sandals
like a shrewd cat, along the roofs, the moon, a moth rushes out.

Deep blue steam from open pipes in a bouquet,
azure blue blood streams from swollen, copper veins.
From behind a wardrobe, fallen silent from dread,
a spectral solo of sorrow on a clarinet is raving half asleep, can you
                                                    hear it?

An azure current burns like a soul inspired,
and the whisper of madness rocks two hearts
from beneath the bottom of consciousness.
                        And the night—into a furious whirlwind!
And with a deep blue blossom gas goes into the torn rug of silence!

Onto the bed, a boat of splendor and the weariness of love,
the lunar mouse sits down—cynical and bobtailed,
and body with body, interlaced tightly for the last time,
writhes in the insatiable spasms of pain and pleasure.

The deep blue angel of the gas bending over them
crowns them with azure fire, as though with myrtle,
and casts souls, like lilies, into ecstasy,
till they catch fire, like the last drops of alcohol.

December 24, 1935

The blindingly black coal of night, the depth and the mine of a heart,
the bottom of nature—the bottom of a mystery and the deep blue
 womb

                                                    of the sky;
a dream resounds in your ears—a crumpled and torn linen scarf,
and in darkness the singing heart of a telephone rings.

This is the way the forgotten chaos of the world's childhood years
awakens,
from beyond the curtain of consciousness the primeval is looking,
like a lake, the chamber in silver enchants,
the moon broken in two withers on the floor like a blue flower.

And the palms of silence that will embrace everything
husk the dark moon's kernel out of a hard shell.
A snub-nosed angel counsels the girls, and time crumbles the
 statues,
only the trumpets of megaphones shine like black tulips.

January 4, 1936

Like a brown linen cloth, a cloud of ravens
settles on lumpy roofs,
and the moon, raising up its blue arms
like a prophet began to curse the city.

For all its sins and trespasses,
for its vanity, betrayal and depravity,
for crimes with which the lair
of scorn is filled with the rabble.

Then reprobates and harpagons
began to sing psalms of atonement.
Calibans clanged bells and
Hataeras neighed like mares.

Loathesome, shameless, dead
luesas rose from their beds
and the victims of proud Sardanopolis
sharpened their red tongues.

Like twelve arrows from the sling of the sky,
twelve winds are sent to the ground,
and the Earth opened the maws of ravines,
and the circle of the Sun broken piecemeal.

An underground crackling from the distance thunders,
a storm of bells strikes the walls,
and the city rolls into an abyss
to the clatter of wings and megaphones.

January 4, 1936

The way a lid covers a chest, the night covered the anthill of the city,
in the valleys of oblivion the bitter almonds of dreams grow.
Stars fall down like leaves onto the heads of the city dwellers,
in spasms of pain and opulence the human maelstrom has fallen asleep.

Weeds of roofs, a singing herb, a powerful bush—antennae.
Lovers, like hot intoxication, intertwine for the night.
Red crabs of lamps crawl along the furniture and walls,
your body grows cold in sleep, the soul rots and mold turns silver.

A red-haired lover in a warm bed and a star in a briefcase,
old feather beds, wet hollyhocks and larvae from books.
At the radio station an inspired speaker places the tiny cold disc
of the moon onto the gramophone of night.

May 20, 1935

Like bits of broken stars, motionless cars sleep at auto cemeteries,
the red blossom of mold measures years and moments frozen in
    brass,
and only the unknown solar orb sways like an eternal truth,
that is also unknown and unfathomable for us, like the blue spirit of
                                          gasoline.

It happens that people, like jackals, disturb the metal corpses in sleep,
and set out the wares of their greed, and thirst, and needs, as though at
                                a bazaar,
and the dead torsos in the deep blue of nights become the sinful beds
of the homeless love caresses of posers and sluts, in whom the stars of
                          evil pour in intoxicating fumes.

The way we dig up the bones of lizards beneath the cliffs of forgotten
                                    centuries,
some day they will dig up metal bones at the cemeteries of our cities.
Girls with nameless flowers, palm trees bear bread, green rue,
and new cities with plazas made of azure, where fire-lions swing.
And unsettled shades, never-silent phantoms rise from beneath the
    earth,
                         the plazas, the grass.

Metropolis,
with the hands of red walls, bring peace to the winged souls of cars!

November 5, 1935

128

Hundred-storied stone buildings sleep like weary animals,
geographers paint the stars with chalk on the map of the sky,
in the reddish glow of lanterns droplets of rain, like winged sand,
and the moon like a golden cat lies on a sofa at my home.

Dead fish in swimming pools rust, and coal and black roses,
patrons and girls undressed, prisoners in jails and poets.
An orchestra of policemen sadly blows into trumpets and French
    horns,
while the bourgeois god counts the stars, souls and coins.

Beneath the city, as though in fairy tales, whales, dolphins and
    tritons live
in water thick and black as tar, a hundred of them in awful cellars,
ghostlike ferns, griffins, drowned comets and bells.
"O thicket made of stone, when will the next flood sweep you away?"

May 1, 1936

Who needs your words?
Someone who weighs bread and salt,
or someone who charges interest,
or someone who during a sleepless night
prints rebellious declarations,
or someone who burns in a fever
or someone who is already desperate from hunger,
or someone who knocks over black prisons,
                    or someone who guards the prisons?

PART VI

From Poetry Not Published
in Collections

Silver chestnut trees bloom again on a path on a Striy Park alley,
you newly want to proclaim to everyone:
just peer around with an open heart,
luxurious spring floats far and widely pealing for seven miles.

The sun will light up luxurious roses in the cities like streetlamps,
the gardens will splash in flowers, in flames of living sparks.
Again the early gust of spring, always healing for everyone,
will charm me and again cast a spell.

The day is crystal, translucent, and the morning is ash-gray in the dark.
No, even though you want to, you just can't curse life any more.

March 27, 1933

The green god of plants and animals
teaches me an intoxicating faith,
the religion of vernal nights,
when the most ancient of elements seethe,
and everything is immutable in eternal change.

(The religions of seething nights
when plant storms thunder).

The green god of flourishing and growth
will rub my bones into dust,
so that a green body of intoxicated plants
will grow and seethe.

Who are you who bows the brows of dust clouds,
fire, a god, a bird, or a storm?

March 14, 1936

A PRAYER

Teach me, flora, growth,
thriving, seething, getting high.
With the primal word, as though with a simple seed,
let me strike essence in the way of a bird with its warbling.

Teach me, flora, silence,
so that I become strong as mighty rivers,
when the moon of unearthly music
will rock them to sleep.

Teach me, flora, happiness,
teach me to die without sorrow!
I accept the sun like communion,
with besotted and arrowlike prayer.

Let the sun—the primal god of all religions—
golden-feathered and life-sowing,
bless my winged home.

I will trace its unearthly gaze,
its sacred, mysterious, Aryan symbol,
I will trace it on my home
and will already be sleeping peacefully.

March 14, 1936

From the Collection
A Welcome to Life (1931)

PART VII

From the Collection
A Welcome to Life (1931)

The water gurgles burbles gurbles burgles,
playing melodies on a flute of stone.
and in a wave-maned attack of white foam,
the tiny jowls of fish blossom from the bottom's depth.

One of them leapt out above the surface
and fell from its flight dazzled by the wheel of the sun.
Since then it is in the sound of the waves
lonely and mute, even though it is still young . . .

Poet! Your black path, a black furrow,
will not soothe the marsh of dampness, the strange rust
of a hitching post, the dry decay of fungus.

You weave the silver thread of your dreams,
You look up like that mad fish
that at least once took a glimpse of the sun.

There is a world high up above us that is:
without storms, clouds, blizzards, thunder, or hail,
that on a summer day betrays the grains,
that beats into the eyes of flowers like a cudgel.

The intense heat of mid-day fails to burn,
just the silence there has boundless power,
and does not allow the ravenous tornado to rage,
and whispers mute fairy tales with silence.

But no one can live there,
because the fierce cold burns worse than lightning
and all of a sudden will break the strongest of wings.

A colorless streak of gray muddles reason.
This way life without storms, struggle, and fatigue
would crush us with silence and frost.

The July linden honey glistens
sticky and glittering in a white pitcher.
In it the stars have melted at dawn along with
the fragrances of flowering bouquets of meadows.

Above a fragrant golden lake
a tiny bee buzzes.
Its shadow lies in a dark thin stripe
on the moist ripple of a yellow brow.

Like a flower, it bends over, besotted with sugar,
petals of wings, the thick liquid
tightly grabs tiny feet.

And with tiny wings the fever of despair begins,
above them the honey has closed up like lips.
Your own happiness sometimes kills you this way.

AUTUMN

The long days ripen like spring apples,
leaves stream from the lindens,
the creak of a wagon flows,
the cry of a finch pours out in a circle near the forest.

The deck of the sky burns at sunset,
from a flock in the aftergrass,
grayish-blue gloom,
in the manger of a ravine a bright aster irritates a hawk.
A drunken piano on the pianoforte of the grass
the wind began to play.
Unequal days ripen all the less
the cocks crow come midnight
and
prickly plants, black poplars
the swarm of wasps
and there
it's already autumn
and

o

autumn
tumn
mn.

Four parallel lines on the map of the heart,
a quadrangle of joy and pain,
four straight lines up to the side that has no name,
that enters as a wedge—between feelings and freedom.

No matter, no matter, the sharp arrow's head cuts the soul,
the crescent moon and veil are ours for a brief night.
Though I know that the husks of words will cover the kernels,
I place the quiet of my lips into the box of a strophe.

In the mountains where, closer to the sun, I first gazed at the sky,
something strange and unknown awakened in me,
and my head lifted up and green words came to my lips.
Now—wherever I might be and whenever,
I am a tipsy child with the sun in my pocket.

And when I descended from the mountain to the noisy cities,
in poverty and failure, I never cursed my fate or gave reproach,
I peacefully gazed at hurricanes of opposing waves.
My songs are a guelder rose bridge over the river of time,
I am a pagan in love with life.

Both a day and a century pass the same. The moments
can't be stopped. Each moment gives birth anew to another,
the first sleeps in the second, both of them in a third, and, like a
    tower,
time grows tall without bounds and makes us mute.

Thus our fate hangs like a draped linen cloth
on the shoulders of the past and future.
We are single links of a chain,
we are but a tiny cut out from the ribbon of time,

This is the usual path of our days,
nothing falls to the water of oblivion.
We must give to life with all our might,
everyone must do this while they are young.

The flower of reality still blooms with hope,
the tree of disenchantment has not yet cast its shadow.
Though it knows there will be frost, the heart nevertheless keeps
    faith
and does not gauge the benefit of truth by crude measure.

For young shoulders the load of the sky is light,
a yawn will not appear to us in monotony.
Oh, not with the words of lips, but with the words of hands
we will sing our song on the threshold of life.

Welcome life! That gives pain, and happiness,
and beauty, and sadness, and grief. My youthful fire has not yet died
    in me.
Welcome life! And I will bring you my soft heart,
forged in steel armor to greet you.

General Index

Index of Poem Titles in English

Index of Poem Titles in Latin and Ukrainian

IN LATIN

IN UKRAINIAN

About the Author

BOHDAN IHOR ANTONYCH (1909–37) was born in the mountainous Lemko region of Poland and grew up speaking the Lemko dialect of Ukrainian as well as Polish. After mastering literary Ukrainian during his studies at Lviv University, he began a formidable career as a poet, publishing five books of poetry from 1933–1937, before his untimely death at age 28.

About the Translator

MICHAEL M. NAYDAN is the Woskob Family Professor of Ukrainian Studies at The Pennsylvania State University in State College and a well-known translator of Ukrainian literature. He has published over 50 articles on literary topics, more than 80 translations in journals and anthologies, and translated or co-translated over 40 books. One of his most recent translations, co-translated with Alla Perminova, is *Zelensky: A Biography*.

About the Introduction Author

LIDIA STEFANOWSKA is a professor of Slavic literatures at the University of Warsaw in Poland. Her doctoral thesis was devoted to the poetry of Bohdan Ihor Antonych, and she is the author of *Antonych, Antynomii* [*Antonych, Antinomies*], a deep analysis of the poet's work.